# For the Time Being

# For the Time Being
Ethnography of Everyday Life

Richard Quinney

State University of New York Press

Excerpts from "East Coker" in FOUR QUARTETS, © 1943 by T. S. Eliot and renewed 1971 by Esme Valerie Eliot, reprinted by permission of Harcourt, Brace & Company. Lines from "East Coker" from *Four Quartets* in COLLECTED POEMS, 1902–1962 by T. S. Eliot. Reprinted by permission of Faber & Faber.

A poem by Ryokan, translated by John Stevens, in *One Robe, One Bowl*. Reprinted by permission of Weatherhill Inc.

Lines from a poem by Ernesto Cardenal in *A Merton Celebration*, edited by Debra Patnaik, Ave Marie Press, 1981. English version from "Death of Thomas Merton," translated by Robert Pring-Mill, in *Marilyn Monroe and Other Poems* by Ernesto Cardenal, published by Search Press, London, 1975. Reprinted by permission of Search Press Ltd.

Lines from "For the Time Being: A Christmas Oratorio" from W. H. AUDEN: COLLECTED POEMS by W. H. Auden, edited by Edward Mendelson. Copyright © 1944 and renewed in 1972 by W. H. Auden. Reprinted by permission of Random House, Inc. Lines from "For the Time Being" in COLLECTED POEMS by W. H. Auden. Reprinted by permission of Faber & Faber.

Lines from "Grief," by Paul Durcan. Copyright © Paul Durcan. Reprinted by permission of the author.

Lines from "Light Turnouts" from HOTEL LAUTRÉAMONT by John Ashbery. Copyright © 1992 by John Ashbery. Reprinted by permission of Alfred A. Knopf Inc.

Production by Ruth Fisher
Marketing by Dana E. Yanulavich

Published by
State University of New York Press, Albany

© 1998 State University of New York

All rights reserved

Printed in the United States of America

No part of this book may be used or reproduced in any manner whatsoever without written permission. No part of this book may be stored in a retrieval system or transmitted in any form or by any means including electronic, electrostatic, magnetic tape, mechanical, photocopying, recording, or otherwise without the prior permission in writing of the publisher.

For information, address State University of New York Press, State University Plaza, Albany, NY 12246

**Library of Congress Cataloging-in-Publication Data**

Quinney, Richard.
    For the time being: ethnography of everyday life / Richard Quinney.
        p. cm.
    Includes bibliographical references.
    ISBN 0-7914-3851-1 (hardcover: alk. paper). — ISBN 0-7914-3852-X (pbk.: alk. paper)
    1. Quinney, Richard. 2. Spiritual biography—United States. 3. Spiritual life. 4. Sociology. I. Title. II. Series.
BL73.Q55A3 1998
973.92'092—dc21
[B]
                                                                                           98-25981
                                                                                              CIP

10 9 8 7 6 5 4 3 2 1

This book is dedicated to my father, in remembrance

> In the meantime
> There are bills to be paid, machines to keep in repair,
> Irregular verbs to learn, the Time Being to redeem
> From insignificance.
> —W. H. Auden

# Contents

|      | Preface | xi |
|------|---------|----|
| I.   | A House in Town | 1 |
| II.  | In a Native State | 17 |
| III. | As the Days Go By | 31 |
| IV.  | Once My Father Traveled West to California | 81 |
| V.   | The Loneliest Sound Is the Whistle of a Train | 113 |
| VI.  | The Professor, a Portrait | 141 |
| VII. | Requiem for the Living and the Dead | 175 |
|      | About the Author | 187 |
|      | Acknowledgment | 189 |
|      | Bibliography | 191 |

*Preface*

Now that this work has been completed, a few words with the advantage of hindsight can be offered. A foreword that is possible only afterward.

This book from start to finish, if nothing else, is a study in the passing of time. And it is the passing of the writer in the course of time. We who remain as readers—you and I—imagine another time and another place. We then move on to what is to come next.

Before us is a book, an artifact of a lived experience, a document of a life lived in the course of a decade. The writing—the process of writing—was part of the living. In some cases, the writing was the living, and made the living possible.

You will note the changes that take place during the writing, and recognize that all is impermanent and that nothing remains the same. Even the philosophy, the basic sensibility of the book, is altered from beginning to end. What began as mystical experience turns into an existential understanding of everyday life. The book survives as a document of the close watch given to this life. All of this, of course, in connection to those with whom we live most intimately.

The universal is in the particular. Or, better stated, all that we can know of anything that might be imagined as universal is known in the particular, in this everyday, mundane life. True, we are all part of one another, interconnected beyond the separations made by the mind. But as a writer, I give you the world as experienced by this single individual. And even when I am moved to generalize beyond my own experience, be cautioned that this is just one observer writing to make sense of his own life.

I want to quote D. H. Lawrence. Writing his book of travel essays, *Mornings in Mexico*, in the 1920s near the end of his life, Lawrence made observations about his project. I am touched, emotionally and intellectually, each time I read the opening words of his book. Writing about the act of writing, he begins:

> One says Mexico: one means, after all, one little town away South in the Republic: and in this little town, one rather crumbly adobe house built round two sides of a garden patio: and of this house, one spot on the deep, shady veranda facing inwards to the trees, where there are an onyx table and three rocking-chairs and one little wooden chair, a pot with carnations, and a person with a pen. We talk so grandly, in capital letters, about Morning in Mexico. All it amounts to is one little individual looking at a bit of sky and trees, then looking down at the page of his exercise book.

Lawrence then reminds us that when books come out with grand titles like *The Future of America* or *The European Situation* we should remember that a person, in a chair or in bed, is making little marks on paper with a fountain pen. And Lawrence writes:

> Still, it is morning, and it is Mexico. The sun shines. But then, during the winter, it always shines. It is pleasant to sit out of doors and write, just fresh enough, and just warm enough. But then it is Christmas next week, so it ought to be just right.

Always, the solitary writer trying to make sense out of the world at hand.

Throughout my book are lines repeated from W. H. Auden's oratorio poem titled "For the Time Being." As a mantra that runs through my book: The time being is all the time we have.

It is the most trying time of all. We seek daily to redeem it from insignificance. Thus the attention I give to this everyday life.

This everyday life of ours, as Henri Lefebvre noted, is "the most universal and the most unique condition, the most social and the most individuated, the most obvious and the best hidden." Anything else that exists arises from the everyday. Although we live in a historical era in which all aspects of everyday life are mediated by the logic of commodities, everyday life is the source of social change and transformation. Everyday life is, indeed, of consequence. The lived experience—shared with others—is our social reality. And it is the only reality we can know.

We work, we play, we sleep, we love, we walk the streets from place to place—such an ordinary existence. But if we let the ordinary escape our attention and our care, we miss life itself. Much, in other words, depends upon the mundane. Any sense of the extraordinary is grounded first of all in ordinary experience. With imagination, the mundane and the sublime are one. An objective of this book is to give witness to the special qualities of everyday life. The meaning of our existence is in the details of being alive. For the time being is everything.

I call my account of everyday life an ethnography. I think of myself as an ethnographer, as one who describes a culture, a culture that is the world as experienced by the ethnographer. And within the world that I experience, as James Agee said of his *Let Us Now Praise Famous Men*, I hope to tell everything possible as accurately as possible. Primacy, of course, is given to the telling of the story. Ethnography, for me, is in the telling, is in the writing. Rather than being an adjunct to observation, the writing—the ethnographic writing—is the ethnography. The world of lived experience is observed, described, and interpreted all at once, in the course of the writing. There is no ethnography without the telling, without the writing—without the writer.

Such an ethnography is the story of the life of the ethnographer. My life, much of the time it seems, is lived as an ethnographer. I use the tools at my disposal to describe and make sense of this life of mine. Camera in hand, I begin the day. With pen and notebook, I make a few words to the day. Perspectives and genres change from day to day as the life is lived. There is no separation between the ethnography and the ethnographer. My ethnography is an autobiographical ethnography.

There is little concern here for the boundaries of disciplines. An ethnography of human existence, an existence itself beyond boundaries, necessarily covers the territory of religion, philosophy, literature, the environment, visual arts, music, drama, literary criticism, sociology, the psychology of the self, and more. In other words, disciplinary boundaries are broken and transcended. Just as in real life, so in autobiographical ethnography.

The reader of any text has a second chance. A chance for an understanding that is brought about by being at a certain remove from the ethnography. A reviewer of the manuscript for my book observed that at the heart of my efforts is the life of my father. There is a close identification between father and son, although the son has spent a lifetime fleeing the Midwest farm of his father and mother, but never being able really to leave it behind. The reviewer suggests that I might think more about the ways the father influenced the son. I have had a life of travel, with camera in hand, remembering all the time my father's one trip to California in 1924. True, in all ways, my father's biography precedes my own.

Throughout the book, I quote extensively from the works of others—poems, fictions, sacred texts, memoirs, literary criticisms, musical compositions, and conversations heard in places public and private. I am fascinated and constantly enriched by this culture that we humans have created, and that we continue to create daily. Our lives are lived daily in this rich and common culture. I hope to make my own contributions to this culture.

As my father plowed the fields, you would often hear him singing. In the barn, milking cows early in the morning, he would be singing "How 'ya gonna keep them down on the farm after they've seen Paree?" The radio would be tuned to WLS in Chicago, country music and the livestock reports. My father had memorized as a schoolboy the poems of the time, reciting throughout the summer, "Barefoot boy with cheek of tan..." Each fall, as we picked corn by hand and threw each ear into the wagon, my father could be heard saying, "The goldenrod is yellow; the corn is turning brown." Often he would recite, "I shot an arrow into the air; it fell to earth, I knew not where." His days on the farm—his whole life—were enhanced by the cultural world around him. He danced, and he had met my mother at a dancehall in town. He carried a camera throughout his life. He was a farmer. This book is dedicated to him.

I now live in town, this prairie town, within easy driving distance of the farm. Trains speed through town, near my house, night and day. I keep my daily rounds. Someday I will move on, one way or another. In the meantime, in the course of my life and labors, I find contentment in a knowledge that comes from being a participant rather than merely a spectator. Knowledge is knowing how to create a home with others. And I am learning that home is a lived relationship rather than a place. One then is free to travel in this world.

Near the end of the book, a character clearly emerges, the one that I call the professor. The one who once professed; the one who has become a wayward professor; the one who waits. His is a simple story; I have great sympathy for this character. Parts of his story were covered earlier in the book when I was giving my own account. His life moves on; someday you will speak of him as the one who once was the professor.

The book ends with a requiem, a requiem for the living and the dead. The hope is that one has lived a good life. In some ways the requiem is a reprise of what has gone before. It is a meditation on this life, a reflection and a source for the life that remains. Even as we live this moment, a requiem is playing in the background. A music that assures us that we live, and a music that makes us grateful for this life. This everyday and wondrous life. For the time being is everything.

# Part I

# A House in Town

The house in which I live lies at the end of a wooded street that slopes down to the river that flows slowly through this prairie town. Crows move among the high branches of the oak trees until sundown. Then they fly west out of town to their roosting places. At night I read a Buddhist poem. There is nothing that has to be reported. I have come to find meaning in the simple things of each day and night.

After several years of being without a place I might call home, living in a house of unrest, in the homes of friends, in the rooms of landlords, I now live in this Cape Cod style house. It has been a year since I moved here, just before the winter holidays. Now, in January, I have lived a full cycle of seasons at home.

Sixty miles to the north is the family farm. It has been nearly a decade since I returned to be near the place of my birth. My mother still lives on the farm. When growing up, I remember my father often saying that someday he would leave the farm and move to a house in town. He died one cold fall day walking from the tractor to the machine shed.

I continue to teach at the university, on the other side of the river, within view of the house. Both my daughters are grown and have left home. The time has come for a life of some retreat. The clouds and the trees and the fence lines will guide my way.

Snow has fallen during the night, leaving a soft cover that glistens in the morning light. Three squirrels play in the tall white pine in the backyard. The day begins quietly, in meditation. I open *The Upanishads* at this early hour and read: "Those who realize that all life is one are at home everywhere and see themselves in all beings." The passage is a reminder of my own quest of the last few years. With care, I am now beginning to look back at—and reflect upon—the years that have brought me to where I am at this moment, in this house in town, on a winter's day.

Tonight I will read again a poem by the eighteenth-century Zen monk and hermit Ryōkan.

> My life may appear melancholy,
> But traveling through this world
> I have entrusted myself to Heaven.
> In my sack, three shō of rice;
> By the hearth, a bundle of firewood.
> If someone asks what is the mark of enlightenment or illusion,
> I cannot say—wealth and honor are nothing but dust.
> As the evening rain falls I sit in my hermitage
> And stretch out both feet in answer.

Ryōkan had reached the stage of an enlightened life depicted in the last of the ten Zen pictures on the search for the missing ox. He goes "to town with helping hands," renouncing worldly goods and personal cares, his only thought being how he can serve others. I will wander downtown along the snowy streets, reminding myself of the paths that others have taken.

***

There came the time, shortly after returning from Ireland five years ago, when matters of spirit and form of life pressed with great urgency. I was in my early fifties, and changes were about to take place. Beginning a new journal, I gave it the title "A Spiritual Journey," noting on the front page: "Toward a life lived fully in the spiritual world—for an everyday life filled with the holy." I will never have a full understanding of the years that followed, nor is one needed, but the experience was one of deep personal crisis—a dark night of the soul. The results were, at least, threefold, altering my spiritual life as lived daily, changing the way of my life and teaching at the university, and dissolving a marriage of thirty years. I am now in need of giving some attention to those years that have brought me to this house. Then, I might live completely—with awareness—the days and nights that remain.

By the time I reached the gates of New Melleray Abbey, a Trappist monastery in Iowa, on a February evening of 1987, and was greeted at the door by Father Samuel, the Guestmaster, I had spent several months in preparation. I had thought of the possibility of a contemplative life, in a monastery, where there might be a safe and caring community, with life devoted entirely to the sacred. All of my reading during these months was given to spiritual works. I was trying to find some peace within, a constant and steady peace, in the midst of daily turmoil. I was informed by Swami Rama in the *Himalayan News*: "We are constantly identifying ourselves with the objects of the world and forgetting our real Self within. To attain peace it is not necessary that we obtain anything new—we simply need to cease identifying ourselves with that which is not ours." Perhaps this peace might be found in one of the places created for spiritual awakening and practice—in an ashram, a mountain retreat, or a monastery.

There was the search for a peaceful environment—related to the natural world, in a loving community—where there could be a balance and harmony in life. Then, as Father Bede Griffiths, living in an ashram in India, suggests, "you are open to the divine and you can experience it day by day, hour by hour in your life."

On a December day, a Saturday with the glow of a mellow light, two months before my monastic retreat, my friend Bruce Von Zellen and I drove to New Melleray Abbey for a day's visit. Driving over the Mississippi and into Iowa, we listened to the tape that our friend Mason Myers had recorded for me several months earlier. The sounds of the Celtic harp, on one side, and Jack Teagarden, on the other, filled the car as we talked about Mason and about his death only the day before. A philosopher who taught at the university up to the time of his death, in his seventies, Mason dwelt not only in words but in the wonder beyond words. One of his favorite lines was from the *Tao Te Ching*: "Existence is beyond the power of words to define." On Sunday, I would read the passage at Mason's memorial service. And from his notebook, I read the last lines he had written, a passage from Dag Hammarskjöld's *Markings*:

The light died in the low clouds. Falling snow drank in the dusk. Shrouded in silence the branches wrapped me in their peace. When the boundaries were erased, once again the wonder: that I exist.

In my own daily existence, I had the overwhelming sense of being separated and abandoned—at home, in my marriage. Love no longer being known in my deepest personal relationship, I turned to a larger world. Bede Griffiths quoted the words of a prior in Dostoevsky's *The Brothers Karamazov*, and in them I found comfort and relief: "Love all God's creation, the whole and every grain of sand in it. Love every leaf and every ray of God's light. Love the animals, love the plants, love everything. If you love everything you will perceive the divine mystery in things." I was being directed to a sacramental life, a sense of oneness with the whole world, an all-embracing love. In suffering, there is an opening of the heart.

Ultimately, it was beyond words and speech, and beyond the self, that a communion with the all of creation was experienced. The original unity was being recovered. Using words to express his own realization of the wordless unity of all, Thomas Merton wrote in his journal, "What we have to be is what we are." Beyond words and concepts, much of life is to be lived in silence and wonder. In my own journal, I write that I will dwell henceforth in the love of the mystery—the nameless. On New Year's day, I resolve that my life—and my work—will be a reflection of that which is greater than myself. May I be a servant, a witness, an example of a life lived daily in the transcendent. May I love completely. I add: Go for walks, live in peace, let change come quietly. Travel lightly.

This morning the fog rises from the snow on the plowed fields at the edge of town. I have just returned from photographing along the country roads. The war in the Persian Gulf goes on, this being the twenty-first day since it began last month. In DeKalb we protest and mourn. Four years ago today I was staying at

New Melleray Abbey as a monastic associate. I have found all the mystery I now need in the living of this winter day.

Having stopped in Dubuque for a last supper at a Greek restaurant, before entering the monastery for a week, I sat alone with a cup of tea at New Melleray as the monks ate their supper in silence. Brother Dennis gave me a brief tour of the monastery, and provided me with a choir tunic for evening Compline. The clock in my assigned room was slow, so that I missed the last Office of the day. At eight, with assurance of no dogs to bark into the night, and the feeling of being in a safe domestic haven, I fell asleep.

Sleeping soundly, I missed the Office of Vigils at 3:15 A.M., and that of Lauds at 6:30. I awoke with an immediate sense of wonder, and shortly Father Samuel knocked on the door, greeted me, and took me to Terce for the reading of scripture and the singing of psalms. I was given a copy of the *Primer on Monastic Spirituality*, prepared by the monks at the abbey, and I returned to my room. The *Primer* informs me that the solitary dwellings of the early desert monks were called by a word that means "one-alone." I am then advised: "If you are to really share in our life as monks, you too must be 'one-alone.' You too must seek God in the solitude of your cell." It is in this room that I might know the contemplative moment of *lectio divina*, a heightened awareness of God, a period of loving attention, "a wordless response to God evoked by His Word." Beyond thought and speech, in contemplation, one "just knows and loves God."

Later in the morning, Father Samuel returns to my cell for a spiritual conference. We talk of separation—from one another, from God—as "sin." "Hell," he says, "is living without love." In losing ourselves in Christ, we find that love. Together, as we talk on, we miss the Office of Sect. After lunch, I walk out into the bright day and photograph patches of snow, the brown fields, a grove of Norway spruce, the limestone buildings of the abbey. A jet trails across the blue sky, and black-capped chickadees search for seeds in the long stubble beside the road.

Browsing in the library, I find a book commemorating the life and death of Thomas Merton. A poem by Ernesto Cardenal catches my attention:

> Love, love above all, as it were a foretaste
> of death.
> Kisses had the savour of death in them
> being
> involves being
> in some other being.
> We only are when we love

But in this life we love only by fits and starts and weakly. We love and we die throughout life; there are the times when we are in a darkness devoid of love. At Vespers we sing Psalms 103, ending: "Let sinners vanish from the earth and the wicked exist no more. Bless the Lord, my soul."

Next morning, the monk in blue and white running shoes helps me locate the pages of scripture as we stand in the choir. This day we will do manual work after the noon meal and the Office of None. I am prepared, having read from the *Primer* that "we work because the work we do is the most effective way we can love and serve our brothers here and now." It is work—in the fields, in the kitchen, in the laundry—that "creates the material substratum and the physical conditions which make the prayer-life possible for our brothers individually and as a community." Under the direction of Brother Hilary, we four monastic associates scrape up wood chips from the cemented barnyard, the wood chips remaining from the monastery's winter fuel supply. After supper—taken individually in silence—the courtyard bell rings, and I put on my hooded tan choir tunic and go down the stone-walled stairway to Compline. Stars shine through the high windows of the darkened church. The tall monk strums a guitar, and we chant "place your trust in the Lord."

While in my room the next day, during the long periods reserved for prayer and contemplation, I give much attention to the heart prayer. "Unceasing prayer is a state of being, a permanent quality of life, an habitual disposition of heart," the *Primer* informs. The Orthodox prayer is offered: "O Lord Jesus Christ, Son of God, have mercy on me a sinner." I create my own heart prayer, "O Lord God, lost in Thy Love," and I repeat it unceasingly, with the in breath and the out breath, during the periods of silent retreat. Leaving the mind with its endless thoughts, feelings, and memories, I know what it is to follow the heart.

On the desk in my monastic room is a framed photograph that Father Samuel has lent to me. It shows Father Samuel drinking beer with Thomas Merton in 1968, in Merton's hermitage on the grounds of the Trappist monastery in Kentucky. In our own refrigerator, Father Samuel has supplied us with bottles of Löwenbräu.

The days go by, and my week's stay at the monastery is coming to an end. I wonder how Thomas Merton would be living his life if he were alive today. Would he still be a Trappist monk, or a Buddhist monk, perhaps, or would he leave the monastic life? I wonder what I should do now: Continue as a professor and teacher? Choose another vocation, in a religious calling? And what about my marriage, and the sources of our separation from one another and of my separation from the divine? What is clear after my week here is that my life is to be given to what Thomas Merton calls, in *The Waters of Siloe*, "the one activity which is the beatitude of heaven." He writes: "That activity is love: The clean, unselfish love that does not live on what it gets but on what is given; a love that increases by pouring itself out for others, that grows by self-sacrifice and becomes mighty by throwing itself away." In this love, "we resemble God, because God himself is love."

It is also becoming clear, given my own particular history of integrating all experiences, that I must live a loving life in active worldly participation. Certainly I do not need the symbolism and the liturgy of the Church; I find the sacred mystery in the simple things of everyday life. Buddhism draws me into the sacred as no other form does. And someday even it may vanish from my practice. As long as there is mystery and as long as there is love, I know unceasingly that which is called God.

The night before my departure from the monastery, I come down with the flu. I am sick all the night, as Father Samuel tends to my needs. In the morning, he comes with fresh linens and offers me a light breakfast. He says that like other monks in the monastery, I am suffering from "the scourge." My getting sick is a bad ending, he observes, but adds, "The Lord moves in strange ways, everything that happens is for a purpose."

Carrying my bags to the car, I think to myself, I will start the ride home, but I know that the way home is somewhere within, and I am still traveling. My journey will be firmly in the mundane world, the everyday life lived in the sacrament of each moment. Thankful I am, as I told Father Samuel, to have experienced the contemplative spirit of monastic life. I drink bottles of cold water as I drive east to DeKalb.

---

That I might love—as a manifestation of being lost in Thy Love—becomes my daily meditation. The monastery has pointed me to the way of the bodhisattva, the mindful living of daily life in the service of others. Now my path will be in the world of everyday life, in the practice of *metta*, loving-kindness. The spiritual, the holy, as I can know and practice it, will be in the simplest of actions—in eating and walking, in working and resting, and in the helping of others. Everything is to be part of the sacramental mystery of existence. In all of my work, as teacher and professor, and in my personal relationships, I will try to bear witness to the holy oneness of all. In a book on Zen, *The Way of Everyday Life*, I am reminded: "This world, this everyday life, is reality, the total, absolute reality. This is where we must look, and this is where we must learn to live the only life we will have."

My own mystical journey, the search for union with the divine mystery in everyday life, continues unceasingly over the following months. Much is experienced in the cloud of unknowing, beyond reason and speculation. The night of darkness has its own illumination within the heart and soul. I am instructed by William Johnston's words in his book *The Inner Eye of Love*: "Love is the motivation and driving force behind the mystical journey—it is precisely love that leads one beyond thoughts and images and concepts into the world of silence. The inner eye is now the eye of love."

Love becomes my guide and points the way during these months. "A time will come," says St. John of the Cross, "when the inner flame will tell you what to do in your daily life." The need for union, the desire for peace in everyday life, the sorrow of this human heart, all these lead to the decision to end my marriage. Although the daily struggle will continue for months, until a final break is completed, a new life course is beginning.

※

The time was one of waiting. "They who wait for the Lord shall renew their strength" (Isaiah 40:31). Of letting things happen in their own time, of letting go. I was informed by the Buddha: "The secret of health for both mind and body is not to mourn for the past, not to worry about the future, and not to anticipate troubles, but to live wisely and earnestly for the present."

I walk with Solveig along the trails of Shabbona State Park on hot summer days, wandering, traveling far—here at home. My daughter Laura is married in Cambridge, in the lounge of Eliot House at Harvard University, taking vows for "a life of truth and kindness." My mother sits in front of the fireplace on Christmas eve. Anne, my younger daughter, prepares to leave home and join her sister. Ambiguity and sorrow. "The darkness and the light are both alike to thee" (Psalms 139:12). I read from T.S. Eliot's "East Coker," a passage beginning "I said to my soul, be still, and wait without hope/For hope would be hope for the wrong thing," and ending "So the darkness shall be the light, and the stillness the dancing."

My heart prayer, as another year begins, continues to be on the mystical union, on the divine and human as one. Trying to keep from grasping, knowing that nothing in this world is secure, I watch all things as they rise and pass away. There is a caring for each moment, beyond the craving thought of the self, a compassionate awareness of all suffering. Fear of an unknown future vanishes when I experience the ceaseless flow of life. One day, I ask for the last time, "What is the meaning of life?" An answer: "Life is in the living of it."

There is, still, a grieving for what is passing. A kind of death. In the living and the changing is the dying. "Our spiritual life," we are reminded in *Seeking the Heart of Wisdom*, "brings us to acknowledge the temporality of life, to accept aging, death, and the temporary nature of even the most beloved people and experiences around us." I am coming to terms with this, in the grieving.

---

A Hindu chant: "The truth is one, we call it by many names." I have known this for many years, yet there is the need for spiritual advice. Father Kaley, at the Newman Center, becomes a guide and counselor. He says that we live according to what we pray to, that our image of God affects how we live. I observe that I had lived for years without the image of a personified God, there being no way we humans can know the existence of such a God. Then the realization, reaffirmed: that which is called God, for me, is the unknowable, the mystery, the oneness of all. I do not know its human name: I call it Love.

My faith is in the unity, the oneness, the interconnectedness of all that exists, the life that is beyond birth and death. I am in the depths of the spiritual when I am in the mystery of things, when I am without knowledge or belief. The spiritual is evident in suffering and in joy, in peace and in justice, when we are without ego, when we are compassionate in our everyday lives. It is the spiritual that unifies a life. Thomas Merton writes, in *Thoughts on Solitude*, and this I copy into my journal, "Your life is shaped by the end you live for. You are made in the image of what you desire." No need to try to answer the unanswerable questions. It is enough to attend to the wonder of our daily lives.

There is little striving left in my life. The search is not what directs my life any longer. Practicing the wonder of existence is what I attend to daily. I realize, with Alan Watts, "that the unknown and the inconceivable is our own original nature." Being aware of my inner workings, and my relationship to all that is, I realize that there is nothing I can do to improve myself. I am as I am. Watts concludes his essay "Suspension of Judgment": "Getting out of your own way comes about only when doing so ceases to be a matter of choice, because you see that there is nothing else for you to do. In other words, it happens when you see that doing something about your situation is not going to help you, and that trying *not* to do anything about it is equally not going to help you. Then where do you stand? You are nonplussed. You are simply reduced to watching, and letting it be."

I watch, and action comes out of my awareness in the here and now. In the words of Zen Master Linji, of an earlier century, "If you attain real, true perception and understanding, birth and death don't affect you—you are free to go or stay." The future takes care of itself. Letting go, lost in Thy Love.

East Lagoon, DeKalb, Illinois

New Melleray Abbey, Peosta, Iowa

West From New Melleray Abbey

University Road, South of DeKalb

Spring is nearing as a day of rain follows a night of snow. Winter wanes on this March morning. The sun will not shine through the gray clouds this day. No birds are in sight. A red squirrel in the backyard eats from the ear of wet corn thrown from the garage. I will walk over the bridge to the library this morning. Dwelling inward, there is wonder about my true being in this vast and mysterious universe.

Last summer, all the days that I crossed the bridge, a large bullfrog sat in the mud below. His single task and purpose, to wait on the procreation of his species. Eventually a smaller companion appeared, and together in the sun at the river's edge they sat motionless throughout the day. Four young bullfrogs poked their noses out of the water as the days of summer ended. Now as I walk over the bridge, I look down through the dark and muddy water, imagining their winter in the bottom of the river. Likely there will be stirring soon.

My reading moments during the last few months have been filled, naturally it seems, with the ancient Sanskrit stories and scriptures of *The Bhagavad Gita* and *The Upanishads*. I had read these works years ago, but recently I found the new translations and commentaries of Eknath Easwaran. In the reading, I discovered a new understanding of the texts, and I found what was important for my living of each day.

Affirmed in the dialogue between Sri Krishna and Arjuna is the reality that pervades the impermanence of each passing moment, of each passing life. Krishna, the divine within, instructs Arjuna: "Realize *that* which pervades the universe and is indestructible; no power can affect this unchanging, imperishable reality. The body is mortal, but he who dwells in the body is immortal and immeasurable." And shortly after, Krishna adds: "Death is inevitable for the living; birth is inevitable for the dead. Since these are unavoidable, you should not sorrow.

Every creature is unmanifested at first and then attains manifestation. When its end has come, it once again becomes unmanifested. What is to lament in this?" Reality is in the eternal, and I can realize the eternal now, this day.

---

The war in the Persian Gulf ended last week. A ceasefire was agreed upon between Iraq and the United States and its coalition forces. A week earlier, as the ground offensive was being waged, we gathered for a vigil, and I recited a line from *The Mahabharata*. In that ancient story, which contains *The Bhagavad Gita*, a family feud between two groups of cousins erupts into a war that leaves millions dead. The mother of one of the factions declares: "When one prefers one's own sons over those of others, war is near." Yellow ribbons tied around tree trunks and on house porches remain today, supporting U.S. troops, over the sons and daughters of others.

A Sunday drive up to visit my mother yesterday. I took her a copy of *Journey to a Far Place*, a product of my fifty-six years of living, and a tale of the mystery of heaven and earth. The writing began at least twelve years ago, when I renewed with urgency the search for a place called home. In the course of the writing, I returned to the Midwest, and here I remain. This is my Walden.

The journal on my desk, opened in the morning light, reminds me to come to attention. It is a bell of awareness, whether or not anything is written on the page. Its mere presence calls me to attention each morning. Looking back to an entry of last July, I reread lines from the eighth chapter of *The Bhagavad Gita*, alluding to that which is beyond even the formless and unmanifested: "Beyond this formless state there is another, unmanifested reality, which is *eternal* and is not dissolved when the cosmos is destroyed. Those who realize life's supreme goal know that I am unmanifested and unchanging. Having come *home* to me, they never return to separate existence." And I am reminded that "this supreme Lord who pervades all existence, the true Self of all creatures, may be realized through undivided love."

Contained in my journal of recent months is the "secret teaching" revealed by Krishna. When there is love, the love of that which we may call God, there is peace, and we know that we will not perish. The purpose of all life is to realize the divine within, to know the eternal in the union with the unmanifested reality of the universe. This is our *native state*, realized daily in meditative awareness. Krishna speaks: "You can know me, see me, and attain union with me. Whoever makes me the supreme goal of all his work and acts without selfish attachment, who devotes himself to me completely and is free from ill will for any creature, enters into me." The morning is followed by a quiet summer afternoon of working in the garden, making some repairs, and cooking supper. We walk to the bridge to watch the bullfrog resting on the river bank, just as the sun is about to set.

Yesterday, in my class on religion, we read portions of *The Bhagavad Gita* on renouncing the fruits of our actions. Increasingly, over the years, my teaching has moved away from any preconceived objective to a teaching that wanders with its own pace, going in Zen fashion, nowhere. What happens each day of class is just what happens. The message of this approach, if any message need arise, is that we do not know where we are going in advance of the actual process of the going. As students, sitting in a circle, we realize that the results of our education may be other than previously assumed, and to the results we are not attached. Life—like education—is indeterminate, or in Zen terms, insubstantial.

Krishna, speaking to Arjuna, advises: "You have the right to work, but never to the fruit of work. You should never engage in action for the sake of reward, nor should you long for inaction. Perform work in this world, Arjuna, as a man established within himself—without selfish attachments, and alike in success and defeat." Our energies are directed to the action, not to the fruits of the action. How could we know in advance what fruits our actions deserve? In surrendering attachment to results, we act in selfless service, in a stilling of the mind and an opening of the heart. We become one with all. Krishna says, "When a person has freed himself from attachment to the results of his work, and from desires for the enjoyment of sense objects, he ascends to the unitive state." In class, as in the rest of life, what remains is to "renounce and enjoy," as one of the *Upanishads* advised long ago.

Walking home after class, I am aware once again of how I have gradually abandoned the desire to know with certainty all that is around me. I experience not so much the desire to know, but the peace of the inevitable mystery of it all. One now lives in wonder, and in the overwhelming compassion that comes from this wonder. Beyond knowing—in awareness—one is united with that which is formless and unchanging in the entire universe. There is, without doubt, eternal life, here and now.

Crossing the bridge against the raw wind of the late winter day, Krishna's cosmic vision comes to mind. It is the vision of the supreme Self, the eternal Lord, the creator and destroyer of this perishable world. In answer to the question, "Who are you?" Krishna replies: "I am time, the destroyer of all; I have come to consume the world. Even without your participation, all the warriors gathered here will die." Beyond the duality of existence and nonexistence, there is that which is changeless and everlasting. Arjuna responds, in wonder: "You are the knower and the thing which is known. You are the final home; with your infinite form you pervade the cosmos." At home, I am fully aware that I will not perish—rather, I will have eternal life.

---

The search for peace in this life continues each day. Years of practice have made me know that home ultimately is to be found beyond the illusion of the self, in the realm of the larger Self, referred to throughout *The Bhagavad Gita*. The teaching is expressed in the Sanskrit words *tat tvam asi*: "Thou art that." The traveler is on the way toward oneness with the eternal Self.

With camera in hand this morning, ready for a day of photographing, I know that the mystery of my true being is reflected in the light of the universe. "Show me your original face, before you were born," a Zen master requests, and I know the answer in the many ways the light falls on all that I experience each day.

Over the years my photographing of the light has changed. For a long time, my favorite time to photograph has been at high noon on bright and cloudless summer days. Only recently have I found an appealing light on an overcast day, early in the morning or late in the afternoon, in the winter, spring, or fall, often between seasons. My being, within the oneness of all, now favors another light.

It is in the light that I find my true place, a home in the world. The light of the natural world is the source and energy of all my being. Within this light, I am an integral part of all that is. There is no longer a separation between the human and the nonhuman, the animate and the inanimate. There is an interpenetration of all things. I am in union with all of creation—and with that which creates.

That I may gain access to the reality of the oneness of all is in the tradition of the visual image—in painting and in photography. This physical eye of mine allows me to see the great wonder of existence, existence itself. I am, as Ralph Waldo Emerson phrased it, "a transparent eyeball." Beyond the ego that separates me from the rest of nature, the eye sees the union of all things. With my camera, the eye that records, I drive down a country road and share Emerson's experience of the moment: "I am nothing; I see all; the currents of the Universal Being circulate through me; I am part or parcel of God." The wonder of the moment is caught in the act of photographing. The photograph is the artifact of that experience, a concrete reminder of a mystical union, a moment of being at home in the light.

In the act of photographing the landscape, the ordinary has become extraordinary. Everyday life and the things of everyday life have become elevated to the transcendent. We are now in the realm of sacred space, where the ordinary and the most mundane things of this world are of sacramental quality. The contemplation of any ordinary thing—through the viewfinder of my camera—is made extraordinary by the very fact of my giving attention, of being aware. Thoreau observes at the edge of Walden Pond, "Only that day dawns to which we are awake." The photograph is a constructed reality formed out of my particular perception and consciousness—the product of an act of love and attention.

And viewing the photograph at a later time is likewise a construction of the imagination brought about by a special awareness. The photograph now has an "aura," a presence that is more than artifice, and I the viewer experience a heightened sensibility in the presence of the photograph. In the black-and-white photograph, light creates and forms the image that comes to my eyes. Looking at the photograph, I am joined with the divine energy of the universe. Roland Barthes studies the photograph of his mother, no longer living. There is something more than the grain of the paper. He observes the photograph and notes, "The effect it produces upon me is not to restore what has been abolished (by time, by distance) but to attest that what I see has indeed existed."

Perhaps it is the transcendence of death that we see in our photographs—and seek in all our photographing. The wonder is in the fact of our existence, and the photograph—made of light—informs us once more that this too existed. And each time I view the photograph, the subject—whether person or something of the landscape—is resurrected and lives again. I, the viewer, live as well, at one with all things.

Thus, in the light, we *see* into the true nature of things. In the course of photographing over these years, I have come to have glimpses of what Zen masters refer to as "true perception." With such perception, Linji noted long ago, "You needn't seek wonders, for wonders come of themselves." Photography takes one to the essentials, beyond thoughts and abstractions. Making the heart open, in love and attention, keeping the mind quiet, you experience a place where words do not apply, and in silence and solitude you become one with the infinite source of light. In photographing the landscape—a simple country road immersed in fog late on a late winter afternoon—I "merge," as Zen master Yuanwu notes, "with the boundless and become wholly empty and still." With camera in hand, life is just that much.

Photographing in the course of this life's journey brings me into harmony with the universe. The primal revelation is that I am of this living earth, here and now, and that I am an integral part of nature. We are of a sacramental universe, every moment of each day and night. My true nature is in the flash and flicker of the light.

※

Every day is a good day when no distinction is made between good and bad. It is thought as much as event that lights each day. Lived in mindfulness, every moment is graced by the sun. I am constantly reminded of this insight. Last December, the *New York Times* told of the long poem by W.H. Auden, "For the Time Being," from his "A Christmas Oratorio." In a season of great expectation, Auden celebrates the sacredness of the mundane in everyday life. "The most trying time of all" is what Auden calls the *time being*. The challenge is to recognize the entry of the sacred into all that is routine and mundane. "In the meantime," Auden writes:

> There are bills to be paid, machines to keep in repair,
> Irregular verbs to learn, the Time Being to redeem
> From insignificance.

Every day is a perfect day, a day of holiness, when no distinctions are made.

It is the distinction between life and death that I seek to erase in my daily living of late. The mind has created the distinction between life and death, a distinction that I now realize is a false one. Life is constant, fixed, ever-present. We are born out of life, and we die into life. The life we know in our conscious being, while we are "alive," is life in its manifested form. Death is but a part of the continuity of life. As Philip Kapleau notes in his book *The Wheel of Life and Death*, "All life is life after death." Nothing is lost in the universe. And the supreme Reality is the void, the formless, the unmanifested—emptiness, that which we call God, that which remains nameless. We are, always, the unborn.

My true being, my *native state*, is a realm where death cannot reach. This is the secret teaching of the Hindu scriptures. In the *Katha Upanishad*, death is the teacher, and we learn:

> When all desires that surge in the heart
> Are renounced, the mortal becomes immortal.
> When all the knots that strangle the heart
> Are loosened, the mortal becomes immortal.
> This sums up the teaching of the scriptures.

When death comes, the body is shed—as in taking off a jacket at the end of the day—and unity with life eternal is completed once more.

In the meantime, in our mortal, manifested form, we seek to end the fear of death. I am instructed by the *Taittiriya Upanishad:*

> When one realizes the Self, in whom
> All life is one, changeless, nameless, formless,
> Then one fears no more. Until we realize
> The unity of life, we live in fear.

There is so much in our mortal lives to which we remain attached. The pleasures we know in our conscious, everyday lives—we want to hold onto these. Beyond all the suffering of being human, brought about by our ego nature, there is the wondrous sense of being alive. But only as I begin to focus on my true nature—beyond birth and death—do I have some relief from the fear of dying.

To live is to die: that is my true nature. In an essay written near the end of his life, Karl Graf Dürckheim asked, and then exclaimed: "How can we attain the life that we ourselves are in the depths of our true nature? Only by dying!" And there is assurance in the sacrifice we humans all must make in our oneness with others. "Physical death may be the supreme sacrifice that anyone can make in life's service—and the whole of life itself can be lived as a sacrifice in the service of others." Our true nature is to live for all others, for plants, animals, and stones as well; to be one with all that is.

This mortal, earthly life is increasingly being lived in a relaxation of the tension between my ego nature and my true nature. I know that my ego nature has a beginning and an end. But in my true nature, there is no birth and no death. There is only life, always and eternal, in my native state. Each day of my mortal existence can be lived with an awareness of my true nature. In my mortal, manifested being is my unmanifested true nature. The formless is in the formed, and the formed is in the formless. As the Heart Sutra instructs, "Form is emptiness, emptiness is form, form does not differ from emptiness, emptiness does not differ from form."

The realization, Self-realization or God-realization, is the movement of my life. Without attachment to the perfect day, without the false distinction between life and death, I exist in wonder and thanksgiving. Loving all creatures of the earth, as myself.

Looking down into the gently flowing river, I see delicate bubbles forming on the surface. Each bubble lasts its time, and disappears into the flowing water from which it came. The life that composed the bubble continues in the flowing river. The bubble has become river. Everything changes, but the river flows on. What is there to gain? Where is there to go? I am with you always. All is as it is. As an eye reflected in the water, now I just watch.

Old State Road, West of Annie Glidden Road

East Clare Road, North of DeKalb

Old State Road, West of Sycamore

Kishwaukee River, Half a Block from Home

Part III

# As the Days Go By

Each day is a move closer to our true nature. The self that has been tied for so long to the ego, seemingly separate from all else, becomes a self that is connected to everything else. The farther we go outward, beyond the ego-self, the more we realize the ultimate within us. And being aware of the mystery in the most mundane things of everyday life, the larger Self of the whole world is realized. It is no longer myself lost in a separate ego, but a Self that is part of everything in this world.

A Sufi, Abu Sa'id, has said, "There is no greater trouble for thee than thine own self, for when thou art occupied with thyself, thou remainest away from God." This is the trouble I face when writing, when I try to put into words my experience of that of which I am an integral part. In the act of writing, we can easily separate ourselves from what is being observed, creating a dualism that exists only in the mind—and in the writing. In the thinking and in the writing, one can actually enhance the illusion of a separate ego. By writing about the everyday, there is the danger of becoming solely occupied with the ego-self's experience of the world. Where, then, is there room for the larger Self, for that which is known as God? How am I to live and to write in a way where there is a return to the world?

Thomas Merton raises the question in his autobiographical writing. He seems to be asking, as in a Zen koan, "How does one write about the self so that the self disappears?" One answer Merton gives, as his biographer Michael Mott notes, is simply "by exhausting the subject of self." Yet, if we are to examine our lives, how are we to live without always being self-conscious, separating ourselves from the living of it? Merton writes: "Life is not futile if you simply live it. It remains futile however as long as you keep watching yourself live it." The problem easily produced by autobiographical writing—that of reinforcing a separate self—can be met only in transcending the problem. The answer to the koan of the disappearing self, in the course of writing, is to become one with what is being experienced and written about. Total abandonment, communion.

The one who now lives and writes about the living, lives and writes to recover the original unity. Not my will be done, but thine. Not my suffering, but *the* suffering. Not my joy, but *the* joy. Writing is but an extension of life lived in oneness with all. Writing is to enhance that oneness.

It makes sense to write sometimes in the first-person plural, rather than in the singular. Such writing indicates a perspective that obviously is more than private, more than ego-centered. Rather than writing "I watch the sun rise," a plural or collective pronoun might be used, "We watch the sun rise." Or the passive voice, without personal pronoun might be appropriate, in spite of the preference of manuscript editors. "The rising sun is watched." The Chinese expression *wuwei*, meaning active passivity, or passive activity, is instructive. Without effort, without a self separated from the action, action takes place. You are, in Christian terms, one with God; your center of being is in God.

Bede Griffiths, in his book *The Cosmic Revelation*, puts it another way. In Hindu terms, he writes, "When you say 'I am Brahman,' what you are saying is that in the inner depths of my being, beyond my ego, beyond my conscious self, I am one with this inner Spirit which is also the Spirit of the universe." With this realization, we write in the course of our everyday life, uniting ourselves with all that is.

When, in the course of the writing, the first-person singular is used, the "I," it is used in the awareness of my true nature. The pen moves, and the mover only appears to be a separate being, remembering always that the writer is nameless, anonymous, one of us all. I watch and write in affirmation of my union with all that is, as the days go by. Not my life, but *the* life.

~

The movement of spring into summer on this day in the middle of May. Three small squirrels follow their mother along the rail fence in the backyard. Playing, they jump from branch to branch in the hawthorn and the elm, and they tumble on the limbs of the tall pine tree. Empty egg shells from the robin's nest have fallen to the ground. Woodchucks now forage in the early afternoon on the bank of the river. I scan the muddy shore below the bridge for the bullfrog's return. Sitting beside the house this morning, with the sun shining through gathering rain clouds, I watch the wren carry twigs to his house in the flowering lilac bush.

Last week Solveig and I were married in the simplest of ceremonies. Our vows, to be good to each other, to love and to care for one another, to be on this spiritual journey together, until death do us part. This week we live in the aura of the reality of marriage at this time in our lives. We know the happiness, even in pain and suffering, that comes in attending to the wonder of the present moment.

Sunday afternoon, at the Buddhadharma Meditation Center in Hinsdale, Thich Nhat Hanh led us in meditation, breathing in and breathing out. He spoke to us on the peace that is in every step. Peace is realized only right here and now in the present moment. We are about to travel.

---

We walked the streets of Paris for seven days and seven nights. Twenty years ago I had tended my daughter Laura as she played in the Luxembourg Gardens. She and I had explored the places that a father and daughter could enjoy together—which could be almost any place that Paris offers. Now, Solveig and I visit my daughter Anne, who is studying at the Sorbonne for the year. On the plane to Paris, I once again read Ernest Hemingway and was reminded: "We always returned to it no matter who we were or how it was changed or with what difficulties, or ease, it could be reached. Paris was always worth it and you received return for whatever you brought to it."

We woke each morning to the sounds of the city. Opening the tall window in our room, at the Hotel Résidence Orsay, we watched the movement of traffic and pedestrians along the Rue de Lille. Morning light danced on the contours of the apartment sity. The places for public gathering are mainly local taverns. We stay home at night, and sometimes meet for coffee during the day in ordinary restaurants. As with most small American towns, this one is characterized by empty store fronts along the main street, real estate speculation, video shops, freight trains day and night, bored teenagers, fast food, motorcycles roaring into the night, high school football, a country club, and contaminated well water. The university is the primary employer in town. Lives, including this one, are spent in one way or another in the shadow of the university.

There is little sense of a community of scholars at the university. Our business is to teach overly large classes of students, publish regularly, and attend department meetings. Certainly this is not a high point in the history of university education, if ever such a time existed. Still, I am a professor, teaching here, now, in my particular way, and this is all an integral part of my life. I lament the personal isolation, the lack of dedication to mind and spirit shown by the institution, the lonely times at the university. Like many of my colleagues, I work mainly at home, and I find satisfactions not granted by higher education today.

I live, in other words, an existential life of bare existence. That is the reality, the reality when I am fully aware. A sense of unsatis-factoriness comes only when meaning is sought beyond this everyday life. All the meaning possible is found in the wonder of a simple existence. I have chosen to live in this town for the existence it provides. I give attention to the living of this day.

The gates have lowered over the highway and the Chicago & North Western freight train speeds toward Chicago. The whistle blasts repeatedly, and I am awake and alive.

Tuesday, July 23, 10:00 A.M.

Sitting this Tuesday morning in the public library. I have come to the accustomed table at the east end of the long reading room. The sun—following a night of thunder showers—filters through the elm and into the large-paned window behind me. Leaf shadows dance across the table and onto my writing pad.

Rose marble columns rise from the floor of the lobby to the skylight above the check-out desk.

The elderly woman with the knitted beige cap, who comes to the library daily, has piled books over her laundry in the shopping cart and has begun reading in the stuffed chair near the fireplace. Several of the homeless, forced from their shelter for the day, are settling into the library. We are here to pass the morning.

I thought that I would quote some lines from my weekend reading of Aldous Huxley. At the end of his last novel, *Island*, Huxley noted the simple facts of a personal metaphysic:

> The fact that the ground of all being could be totally manifest in a flowering shrub, a human face; the fact that there was a light and this light was also compassion.

Nearing death, in the darkness of being blind, the fact of enlightenment remained for him. The extraordinary—the transcendent—is to be found in the mundane, the everyday, if it is to be found at all.

I will wait here in the library, mainly watching, being still, until Solveig comes to pick me up. I plan to be with her at the clinic while she undergoes a minor outpatient procedure. If there are clouds and the light is right, I will photograph this afternoon, at the end of Pleasant Street.

Thursday, July 25, 11:45 A.M.

Stopping for a glass of Killian's Red at Sullivan's. Bratwurst and Italian beef sandwiches are featured today. I have been photographing along Lincoln Highway, downtown DeKalb. A morning of good work. Clouds float high above the highway as traffic goes east and west. A semitruck loaded with squealing hogs passes by, on its way to the stockyards. I am the Watcher.

The morning papers report the arrest of a man in Milwaukee, a former worker in a chocolate factory, who admits to murder and cannibalism. The dismembered bodies of several victims have been found in his apartment. He has turned over to the police Polaroid photographs of the victims, photographs taken while they were still alive, after he had killed them, and of their heads and body parts after he had dismembered them. Before and after shots. Monet's paintings of grainstacks at different times of the day. Yesterday I photographed clouds as they rose and passed away. Care is to be taken as we attend to the mystery of time.

Monday, July 29, 3:00 P.M.

Waking from an afternoon nap, after a morning of traveling by foot uptown and doing some research in the public library. A walk in the morning, in one direction or another, is always necessary for the purchase of the *New York Times*. And a nap following lunch, after reading the *Times*, is often taken, always with pleasure.

For thirty years, my days have been measured by the reading of the *New York Times*. There have been few days without the *Times*. When visiting friends and relatives, in whatever part of the country, and in the remotest of places, I have sought the elusive morning paper. I have walked railroad tracks, driven the roughest of roads, taken buses, to find the *Times* of the day. I know that "All the News That's Fit to Print" is from the perspective of an establishment journalism, and that I must go to alternative sources. Nonetheless, it is the *Times*, over all these years, that has provided me with a personal sense of continuity in this world.

And once the paper is found, it is to the obituaries that I first turn. Friends have questioned this habit, wondering whether there might be a morbid curiosity. And yet, I find delight in knowing who has been with us, what that life has been, and (as the *Times* always reports) how that mortal life came to an end. Many people who appear in the obituaries I have lived my life with—in the news, in the artistic and scientific realms of the culture—and they are passing on. They have come to the same ultimate end. I read the obituaries and I am enlightened.

Last week the *Times* contained the obituary of Isaac Bashevis Singer, the noted writer of Yiddish stories. Today's paper reports on the funeral, which was held at the Riverside Memorial Chapel in Manhattan. We are told that there was little display of grief at the funeral. In his eulogy, the rabbi observed that Singer had convinced those who knew him that "the human spirit does not end with physical death," that "every soul who ever lived is here in one way or the other."

Each morning, in one way or another, I travel in search of the *Times*. What I find is always of eternal consequence.

Tuesday, July 30, 9:30 A.M.

A short time ago, my friend Paul Buhle, living in Providence, Rhode Island, wrote to me about his continuing reaction to the landscape of his birth and early years, that of central Illinois. Commenting on one of my photographs of the land south of DeKalb, he lamented the human isolation in the universe of corn and soybean fields. "It is not a natural thing to be quite so lonely," he observed. He then added, "but yet anything human is natural, and tells us something about our nature." With these lines in mind, I drove south of town last evening before sunset to photograph this Midwest landscape, to be immersed in the corn and soybean fields. The light of the evening sky created infinite shades of green and yellow, and dark shadows played among the rows in the fields.

For those of us who have returned to the Midwest, and for those who have never left, the apparent sparseness of the landscape is a spiritual source at the same time that it isolates us from each other. The landscape is our lesson. It is the text—a riddle as in a Zen koan—that prompts us to be in the world in a special way, to be in the world but not completely of it.

The isolation experienced in the Midwest landscape is an opportunity for solitude. It is the solitude—spiritually experienced—that Henry David Thoreau knew in a cabin at the edge of Walden Pond. Thoreau wrote: "I love to be alone, I never found the companion that was so companionable as solitude." The solitary mind, he observed, is a mind that is at home with itself because it is aware of its relation to everything else. This is also the mind of the desert fathers of the fourth century, made known to us by Thomas Merton, of those "lost in the inner, hidden reality of a self that is transcendent, mysterious, half-known, and lost in Christ." "To leave the 'world'," Merton wrote, "is to leave oneself first of all and to begin to live for others." In solitude, rather than in isolation, we lose ourselves to the higher Self, to everything that is. I am of the whole world.

I have lived a life formed and molded by this landscape. As a child on the farm, a few miles to the north of where I now live, I was an intimate part of the landscape. This landscape continues to be of sacred quality, where the woods and fields and sky measure the depth and breadth of my existence. I look toward the horizon as the evening sun is about to set, and know all the wonder of the world. I am at home.

Wednesday, July 31, 11:30 A.M.

High summer, and August is about to begin. Sartre said that "existence precedes essence." His character Roquentin, in *Nausea*, is suddenly overcome when picking up a pebble on the seashore, seeing through the essence of the stone to the pure fact of its existence. This morning as I sit beside the pool, in Hopkins Park, all things around me, including this self, seem to exist beyond all appearance. And yes, there is a sense of being overcome. How much existence are we willing or able to tolerate?

My camera, as usual of late, is near at hand. In fact, I now carry with me a small autofocus camera purchased last Saturday on a trip to Chicago. A record can be made of things that actually exist, or have ever existed, irrespective of their essence or meaning. The photograph is a document of existence. It is an artifact, as well, of my own existence. I was there, and I too existed. A reminder that everything, ultimately, is the stuff—the suchness—of pure existence, of the unfathomable and mysterious universe. Beyond form, beyond appearance, beyond this life itself, is what we uneasily call Nothing—bare existence.

Sitting at a table under the large umbrella beside the pool. A warm breeze blows in the late morning. The temperature is to reach ninety degrees today. I will go into the water soon, relying on a side stroke to take me across the pool and back again. Growing up on the farm, there was little time to practice swimming, leaving me to this day with a minimum of skill in the water. I feel like the four-year-old boy who just walked by, stopped beside me, peered into the pool, and exclaimed: "Holy smoke! This water's deep. It drowns me all the time." This morning, babies are being instructed in the water, and women lie sunning on the deck.

On the telephone last night, my mother asked again the question she has raised a number of times this summer. "Won't you be glad when school starts and you have something to do?" I explain to her that the school year, when I am "working," is much the same as the summer. Each day is a creation. This is my work, the experiencing of existence, each day and night.

I will immerse myself in the water as the hot sun beats down on the inviting pool. But who would not admit, in the bareness of this existence, some sense of strangeness this morning at poolside?

Friday, August 2, 11:30 A.M.

Beside the pool again, this morning, at the table with the umbrella. My doctor lies sunning in the lounge chair further down the deck. His day off. Humid, overcast, and already in the nineties. I will stay here until later in the afternoon, when I will return home to meet with two former students who are coming to visit from afar.

This summer I have thought much about photography. And I have spent many days out photographing. My aims are quite simple, although I am informed by various treatises on the photographic art. I photograph primarily as another way of recording everyday life: To document our existence, what is, here and now. There is deliberation in the process. In fact, it is deliberation that makes photography "art." Photography is an art the same way the living of everyday life is an art, where life is created each day with attention, with love, with deliberation. I think of Thoreau, observing that I photograph, as he went to the woods, "to live deliberately, to front only the essential facts of life, and see if I could not learn what it had to teach, and not, when I came to die, discover that I had not lived." Everyday life, including the taking of pictures, is an art when carried out deliberately.

My photography is in the perennial style, as Robert Adams terms it, in his book *Beauty in Photography*. I work within the bounds of "straight photography." But this is to recognize, also, that the vision of the photographer, as beholder, selects the subject and frames it in a particular way. My photographs, like anyone else's, reflect my sense of order, my sense of the structuring of nature, my autobiography.

All of my photographs, whether of the prairie landscape or the streets in town, are of nature. And when I photograph, all the nature of human evolution, as *homo sapiens* ("the wise human being"), comes together. My mind, my soul, my being, all coalesce when I go photographing, when the nonverbal image is framed in the viewfinder, and the shutter release is pressed. It is then that I know my true self. There is a moment of great relief.

The resulting photograph, viewed much later, bears witness to the alchemy of the photographic moment. It attests to the experiencing of existence, proves that life has been lived with deliberation, at least for the moment. And that moment is eternity.

Enough talk of photography. Time for a swim.

Wednesday, August 7, 10:00 A.M.

We are reminded that for the ancients, as for contemporary seekers, the world was alive with spirit. The surrounding landscape is infused with the divine, just as our daily life is spiritually infused. The editors of a little book of *Earth Prayers* write of the inseparability of spirit and matter:

> While the distinction between spirit and matter is valid, no one can separate the two, no one can draw a line between them. Spirit and matter are not two different realms of reality, two different layers of the universe.

One and the same reality will be material or spiritual depending on how we approach it. No matter where we immerse ourselves in the stream of reality, we can touch the spiritual source of all that is natural.

All things of this daily life, of this earth, share the reality of the eternal.

This morning I was awakened at five by the cawing of the crow in the maple tree. Going to the window, I watched the crow as it suddenly flew down and brushed against the house. A cardinal sang loudly, *whoit, whoit, whoit*. The early morning light was soft, and a gentle rain soon began to fall. After making a cup of coffee, I went back to bed and slept for another hour.

All seems to be in order this morning. Few people are in the public library. The books rest on the shelves; a librarian is at the desk. I am enjoying the reading of E.B. White's account of his life on a farm in Maine fifty years ago, *One Man's Meat*. Laura and her husband leave today for Tokyo to present papers at a Shakespeare conference. Anne is completing her summer as a counselor at a Unitarian camp in the Adirondacks. My former wife has moved from town, returning to her home state of North Carolina. Solveig and I are driving up to see my mother on Friday. The Interfaith Network is preparing for a weekend garage sale, in our garage, to provide medical supplies for children in Nicaragua.

I make notes this day, as always, to bring some order to this consciousness. We all are historians of our own personal existence. We observe, record, and preserve the events of our lives. And we are in constant search for the place where we belong. Goethe is often quoted as saying that writers in particular have the disease of homesickness, that writers are searching for a place they can call home. Perhaps writers suffer from a paradox: that the search, the analytical separation of the self in the process of writing, makes home problematic. But I attempt another way of writing—a meditative writing—that connects the writer to existence. Observing and recording can become the means for being at home.

In writing these notes this summer, I am lost to the world. I am at home. The editors of *Earth Prayers* furnish a poet's benediction for the day:

Let the words of my mouth,
the meditations of my heart
and the actions of my life be as one,
that I may live each day in harmony
with Mother Earth. Amen.

Tuesday, August 12, 11:00 A.M.

I have driven the twenty-five miles over to Geneva this morning. To have banana pancakes at the Geneva Diner. To see Richard Beard's latest exhibit of paintings. To purchase a copy of Mary Morris's travel odyssey *Wall to Wall*. I will sit for a while in Geneva's public library. Others are here, too, hoping for some revelation in the written word.

I have discovered once again the lines from the Chippewa song:

Sometimes
I go about pitying myself
While I am carried by
The wind
Across the sky.

We live the only lives we have right here on earth. But we know there is more, that we are being carried all the time by the wind across the sky. Catherine of Siena is said to have said that all the way to heaven is heaven. This everyday life of ours is the only place that transcendence can be known. There is no destination apart from the journey. The only heaven we can know is in the living of each day and night. Still, we are of the wind that blows across the sky.

Solveig, born in Norway, and a friend, a native of Switzerland, talked in the sun beside the pool yesterday. They talked of the life of the immigrant, recognizing that they are neither of the old world nor of the new. Once an immigrant, always an immigrant, they concluded. Solveig and I talked later about this conversation, and realized that being an immigrant is common to us all. We are all in this world, but not truly *of* it. We have a foot in both worlds, the world of everyday life and the world of the eternal.

Our true home is in the suchness—the nothingness—of existence. I am at home when I have a sense of the eternal in my everyday life. When I realize that I am in both worlds. We are immigrants in a strange land, blown by the wind across the sky. There is nothing to lament—nothing to pity—when our true nature is thus known.

*Friday, August 16, 10:45 A.M.*

The temperature will reach the high eighties today, yet the first stirrings of autumn are in the air. There is a sense that summer is drawing to a close.

Last night before bed, we tried to remove a chirping cricket from the basement. Placing the cricket under an empty paint bucket, and sliding a magazine between the bucket and the floor, we thought that we were about to liberate the cricket from the captivity of the house. Reaching the starry night beyond the door, we removed the magazine from the bucket, and the cricket fell limply to the ground—dead from our efforts at insect liberation.

Whenever I woke up during the night, I felt a sadness for the cricket. Only the night before I had read the lines of Walt Whitman: "I think I could turn and live with animals, they're so placid/and self-contain'd,/I stand and look at them long and long." All the wonder of the universe is contained in the tiniest of creatures. I had read, also, the words of Meister Eckhart:

> Apprehend God in all things,
> for God is in all things.
>
> Every single creature is full of God
> and is a book about God.
>
> Every creature is a word of God.
>
> If I spent enough time with the tiniest creature—
> even a caterpillar—
> I would never have to prepare a sermon. So full of God
> is every creature.

We are all part of the great mystery—humans, animals, insects, flowers, and stones. Brought together finally in pure and eternal existence.

That which we call God is within all of creation, not separate and beyond, but immanent. I think I will begin today to photograph some of the little things. The universe—close-up, and very near. I will listen for the crickets this August night.

Monday, August 19, 9:30 A.M.

A coup is being attempted in the Soviet Union. Today we watch and listen and talk among ourselves. Hurricane Bob moves up the East coast. Our Prairie Sangha met yesterday afternoon. On this day three hundred and twenty-nine years ago, Blaise Pascal died in Paris at the age of thirty-eight. Thanking everyone, and receiving the final blessing, Pascal said, "Que Dieu ne m'abandonne jamais"—"Would that God never abandons me!"

We are told that Pascal accepted his own imminent death, as he had lived his life, as a sacrifice. Life is given so that others may live. His life was devoted to looking into the nature of being, his own being, the being of others, and the being of God. He laid the foundation for the modern theory of probabilities, taught of mystery through the heart rather than reason, and left room for the absurd—the unexplainable—in the existentials of everyday life.

Over the weekend, I read the letters of Vincent Van Gogh. I have hanging in the upstairs hallway a print of Van Gogh's 1888 painting of Marie Ginoux, the owner of the Café de la Gare in Arles where Vincent had lodged for a time. Vincent was shortly to suffer one mental breakdown after another, and was admitted to the hospital in Saint-Rémy, where he continued to paint and write letters to his friends and relatives.

Madame Ginoux had taken ill at the same time as Vincent, and he wrote to her on December 31, 1889: "Personally I believe that the adversities one meets with in the ordinary course of life do us as much good as harm. The very complaint that makes one ill today, overwhelming one with discouragement, that same thing—once the disease has passed off—gives us the energy to get up and to want to be completely recovered tomorrow." In the letter, he writes that we are not the masters of our existence, and that "what matters is that one should learn to want to go on living, even when suffering." He ends the letter: "In my case my disease has done me good—it would be ungrateful not to acknowledge it. It has made me easier in my mind."

In the painting *At the Café*, Madame Ginoux is seated at a table, arm resting on the edge, with a hand to her face, dressed in black. A billiard table is in the background, and customers are sitting at tables along a red wall. A cat sits on the floor, a plate is on the table, a vapor trails across the room.

Matters of illness and death now seem more concrete. Prompting questions: Did I love enough in this life? Did I live well? How am I to live now? A great compassion came over me when the doctor read the results of my physical examination a year ago last December. As with Vincent, much good has been done, and I am easier in my mind. Madame Ginoux watches from the corner of her eye as I pass in the hallway.

Thursday, August 22, 9:05 A.M.

As I sit on the front steps waiting for the librarian to open the door this bright morning, a troubled man in rumpled clothing paces back and forth, repeating "Whoopty, doopty, I don't know how to wait." He soon leaves. Down the street the Greyhound bus pulls away from the station, "Los Angeles" its destination. The morning paper headlines report the failure of the coup in the Soviet Union. Radios are tuned to one analysis after another.

This week's *New Yorker* is carrying excerpts from the journals of John Cheever. In the final entries, Cheever is sick and dying. He is beyond the trips to the hospital, in bed at home, and occasionally pulling himself to the typewriter to make another journal entry.

The reader is drawn to the intimacy of the journal. Cheever sleeps alone, but even in these times is visited briefly by a lover. He watches his wife's rejection; he is happy with the travels of his grown children; he gives an account of the failures, as well as the successes, of his life. And he writes: "My daughter once kissed me and said, 'You can't win them all, Daddy.' And so I can't." This weekend I will drive to Madison, hoping to find a copy of Susan Cheever's memoir of her father, *Home Before Dark*.

What price does a writer, or any artist, pay to achieve a creative work? John Cheever, considering the ultimate matter of loving, writes in his journal, "Such merit as my work possesses is rooted in the fact that I have been unsuccessful in my search for love." Are we to assume that his work has profited from the lack of love in his life? Or, perhaps, is there the possibility that a life is lived short of love as a consequence of the desire to write? Not only the desire to write, but the need to live on the edge so that the sorrows can be experienced and thus become material for the writing.

No generalizations, of course, can be made on the relation between the creative act and the everyday life of the artist. Yet one wonders. The papers this week have carried the reviews of the biography of Anne Sexton. Her poetry was in large part a way of dealing with her own troubled life. But, also, we are informed by her daughter Linda, in Sunday's *New York Times*, that Sexton provoked events in order to gain material for her writing. Specifically, the daughter writes about her mother, "During the period she was sexually abusing me, she was writing a play about a daughter's sexual abuse." The daughter adds that all the members of the family were hurt by having lived with the poet, but that in the honest telling some of the hurt can be transcended.

Anyone who works outside of the home, "artist" or otherwise, likely wonders about the price that is being paid. Wonders about the time that is being given to other efforts, the time that could have been spent at home. I wonder, especially, how my daughters regard their years of growing up at home. I hope that my life as a father has been caring and loving, and can be remembered as such. I hope that I was a creator of the art of everyday life as much as a writer and teacher in the world beyond the home. We are not speaking here of perfection, whatever that might be, but of a life that is remembered with fondness and love.

I do sense a failing in not having been able to have a marriage that provided a secure household for my daughters.

In retrospect, Valerie and I were not able to reconcile our personal differences in a way that would produce a secure family. Our daughters suffered. I am sorry. Would that all acts of creation might be completely successful.

One of my daughters wrote recently, "Daddy, you are the calm and stable force in my life. I love you." And so I have some hope that art and life can be one.

Friday, August 30, 10:05 A.M.

Laura just called from Boston. She was sitting on the porch as the moving van was being loaded. She reminded me with laughter of the song I used to play for her on the phonograph when she was a child, "Waiting for the Moving Van."

Classes began this week at the university. I tell my students in the Peace and Social Justice course that to know the subject we must become one with it, and that in the process of knowing we will be transformed. Yesterday we ended the class with the words of Thich Nhat Hanh: "Life is filled with suffering, but it is also filled with many wonders, like the blue sky, the sunshine, the eyes of a baby. To suffer is not enough. We must also be in touch with the wonders of life. They are within us and all around us, everywhere, any time." We left the classroom with a sense of wonder, attending to the mystery of our lives.

Last evening—while having dinner at a restaurant in Rockford—Solveig and I talked about how we continue to live in the presence of our parents, especially of our fathers who have died. The guilt that I once felt over my youthful rejection of my father dissipated several years ago as I returned to the Midwest and, at the same time, wrote about growing up on the farm. As I became aware that I was very much like my father, that the seeds of life have been transmitted from father to son, I began to forgive both myself and my father for the sorrow we caused each other. And in writing about my father, and our years together, I sensed that he was free to live again.

There is a letter I want to write to my daughters. To mindfully acknowledge the suffering that is passed from one generation to another. All our ancestors and all future generations are present in each of us. And in the center of our human suffering is the love that is known in being together.

Monday, September 2, 4:00 P.M.

Labor Day. This has always been the last day of the Walworth County Fair. The last day of summer. At the end of the day we would load the livestock into the truck for the trip back to the farm, have our last hamburger at the fair, and take one more stroll through the fairgrounds before driving home in the cool of the evening. In the morning, we would have to be ready to begin another year of school.

Day before yesterday—on Saturday—we drove up to the Walworth County Fair. It had been years since I had walked the grounds that once served as a relief from the daily labors of farm life. It was a time of the year when the lure and mystery of the carnival filled my life. I sensed what it might be to escape from the farm, to grow up, to abandon the country of my birth—to leave home.

There would come a time, over ten years ago when I was in my mid-forties, when I would have to think carefully about those growing up years on the farm. I missed the farm, my parents and my brother, and I longed for the life I had lost. I was, in other words, again searching for a home in this world, and life on the farm in the 1940s served as the model for the place I still called home.

I wrote an autobiographical account of those years as if my life depended upon the reflection that comes in such writing. The writing relieved much of the pain and uncertainty I was feeling in midlife. Eventually, with changes in my life, I would be able to find my home.

And now, only occasionally do I think about the past and the years on the farm, or about the years to come. The writing, the intense thought about the past, the reliving, released me to the present. I was being freed to live my life as it unfolded in the present. Walking the fairgrounds this time, I was on a day's adventure with my wife and friends. As evening came to the fair, we drove home to the house in town.

Friday, September 6, 10:45 A.M.

Standing in a Madison bookstore two weeks ago, I read aloud to Solveig a passage from the *Notebooks* of Albert Camus: "Those who love truth must look for love in marriage; in other words, love without illusions." Last night, burdened with some unknown malady of body and spirit, we cared for each other. "More than the fear of death," I whispered, "is the thought of being without you."

It is probable that we meet only the persons in this world we are supposed to meet, or are drawn to meet, in a union that makes us whole. Everything that happens to us on the way is a preparation. Waters on the way to the sea.

Monday, September 9, 10:15 A.M.

The days of summer are gone—although a hot and humid prairie breeze blows through town this morning. Twenty-five thousand students heighten the density of traffic during the day and bring noise to the night. Ambulance and police sirens scream today. The energy level of the community has risen. Structure and discipline encroach upon my day.

This morning I am preparing for a reading of my writings on the search for home, a reading that is to be given next Sunday morning at a gathering of Unitarians. Likely I will preface my reading with an observation a former student made last week about my writing. His girlfriend had given him a copy of my journey book, which I had autographed for him, and the observation followed his reading of the book.

He observed that my writing is touched by sadness. This I already knew, but I was surprised to be reminded. Life is more than suffering; there is joy in each step and in each breath, in the glow of the evening light. Yet, when I tell the story of my daily life, there is melancholy. To write, in other words, for me at least, is to delve into the depths of my existence. The existential nerve is finely tuned to the pathos of existence, even when there is joy in the wonder of that existence.

Who is not overcome by a wave of melancholy when the ultimate questions are raised? Who am I? Why do we exist? What is the meaning of the universe? As soon as the questions are raised, we realize that a human answer is not possible. Our wonder is profound, but so is the sadness. What is required of us, or hoped for us? The cosmic joke is for laughing. We can never know, and yet we keep asking. But for me the laughter comes only after thinking myself into the depths. Thus the sadness in the writing. Now I laugh, and I am awake.

Friday, September 13, 9:30 A.M.

Waiting in the office of the optometrist for an inspection of my glasses. Markings have appeared mysteriously on the lenses. One hopes to see clearly. I will return home to study contact sheets from the film developed over the summer.

In a photograph taken in July, a man begins to cross Lincoln Highway at the intersection of Second Street. He is carrying a package under his left arm. The First National Bank, now vacant, is in the background. On another contact sheet, from the same day of photographing, and further down the highway, the man who owns the vacant bank has emerged from Ralph's News Stand and Trophy House. He is the town's millionaire, and prevalent are the stories of his illustrious past. In the next two shots, he passes the Lotto sign on the side of the building and is about to enter his dilapidated car. Another car waits at the stoplight.

The simplest of snapshots, Wright Morris reminds us, involves us in time's ineffable mystery. The photograph is at once commonplace and unearthly. In the photograph we are witness to a moment that can be nothing other than the eternal present. The figure in the photograph is fleeting, yet still a mark of time's presence, through time's passage. Wright Morris: "The carriage crossing a square, the pet straining at its leash, are momentarily detained from their destination. On these ghostly shades the photograph confers a brief immortality."

I photograph on a July day, and now I study the negative this thirteenth day of September, a Friday, to be reminded of the play of time, of the timeless, and of the eternal present. When I am in the present moment, without past or future, when I snap the shutter of the camera, I am in eternity. And when I look at the negative today, concentrating in the moment, eternity is with me again. It—eternity—is available to us every moment of the day.

Monday, September 23, 9:50 A.M.

This is the day of the Fall Equinox. The moon that has been shining into the bedroom during the last few evenings will be full tonight. The temperature has fallen below forty degrees. Squirrels run and forage in the backyard.

Leaves are drying on the trees, preparing to fall to the ground. I sit in the green chair in back of the house, and watch, and learn. I read a passage by Thich Nhat Hanh, from his book *Peace is Every Step*:

> I asked the leaf whether it was frightened because it was autumn and the other leaves were falling. The leaf told me, "No. During the whole spring and summer I was completely alive. I worked hard to help nourish the tree, and now much of me is in the tree. I am not limited by this form. I am also the whole tree, and when I go back to the soil, I will continue to nourish the tree. So I don't worry at all. As I leave this branch and float to the ground, I will wave to the tree and tell her, 'I will see you again very soon.'"

The wind blows gently this morning. Leaves rustle in the tree before me.

Last week a freshman student asked me why I write. For fortune, for fame? I have been thinking since about the question. For my health, physical and spiritual, most certainly, and for healing. To stay alive, to be alive. These occasional entries are now a thread for me, woven into a tapestry that I know as my life. And I would admit, as well, that I am witness to an experience that, in my telling, others can learn from. As the leaf nourishing the tree.

Monday, September 30, 12:30 A.M.

We are in the surgical waiting room of Kishwaukee Hospital. Solveig is to undergo an outpatient operation in an hour. An attendant gathers information and gives instructions. The warm breeze that blows through town today graced our walk across the parking lot as we entered the hospital a short time ago.

A song on public radio's *Folk Sampler* reminded us last night that we are all here on borrowed time. And that friends and lovers keep us safe and covered. We, in our true being, come out of the unknown and to the unknown return; in the meantime, we are living on borrowed time. A consolation, for certain, while waiting for surgery at Kishwaukee Hospital.

Monday, October 7, 11:00 A.M.

In this world of care, as the sad singer calls it, all things are possible. Wait long enough, a moment perhaps, and something happens. Heraclitus observed that we never step into the same river twice. Time makes a life in this world.

When I moved to DeKalb eight years ago, I was confronted immediately with the idea of retirement. The topic pervaded much of the local discussion; retirement seemed to be the idea by which most of my colleagues lived their lives, whatever their age. The present appeared to be a time in which one's energies were spent in preparation for a future beyond employment, beyond work. I had not lived with such thought prior to the move back to the Midwest. I have since made perfunctory preparations; a modest amount of my monthly check is being set aside in tax-deferred annuities, and someday I will attend one of the pre-retirement seminars the university sponsors. But retirement is not generally the focus of my present being.

There are reminders, nevertheless. At department meetings there are occasional hints, in verbal exchanges, that those of us who have reached our mid-fifties are being moved to the edges of things. Our orientations to matters intellectual and political are getting softer, more humanistic, less empirical and more philosophical. These are traits that are not highly valued in academic life. We are being given the message that retirement time is nearing, if not for our own good, for the good of the institution. I have seen this happen to others over thirty years of teaching in several different universities. Now it is happening to me.

Last week in our department meeting, in a discussion of course requirements, a younger colleague suggested in a passing comment that a meditation course would be an appropriate prerequisite for all of my sociology courses. The comment was made with sarcastic humor, and the intention was to question publically what I am teaching in my courses in the name of sociology. I realize that my colleague's comment arises from his own ignorance of my teaching, and that my being hurt comes from an unnecessary ego. My studied response is one of nonresistance: "But I say to you, Do not resist an evildoer" (Matthew 5:39). To resist, to respond in kind, is to become what one resists. My spiritual practice, rather, is to go beyond the violence of thought, word, and deed. Some level of perfection: "Be perfect, therefore, as your heavenly Father is perfect" (Matthew 5:48). Or as *The Bhagavad Gita* puts it: realize God.

So, I find it increasingly difficult to engage in the debates of departmental meetings, where kindness to one another is not always practiced. Perhaps in a response of nonresistance, a message of right speech, right conduct, and compassion can be given to others. There are forums outside of formal meetings that are more conducive to humane interaction. I will try to be a teacher in these places. Until retirement do us part.

Wednesday, October 15, 10:40 A.M.

Anne has returned to Providence after a five-day visit at home. I am here in the public library this morning reading poems of Paul Durcan, poems inspired by paintings in the National Gallery of Ireland. The word and the visual image come together, enhancing one another, in the exhibition (and the book) titled *Crazy About Women*.

After meeting Anne at O'Hare on Thursday morning, we drove to the south side of Chicago, Hyde Park, the area around the University of Chicago. We browsed in Powell's Bookstore and had lunch at Piccolo Mondo. Posted on a tree along 57th

Street was an announcement that Paul Durcan would be reading his poems in the Theater building at four o'clock. We had met Paul in Ireland five years ago, had talked on several occasions, and had corresponded.

A pleasure it was to see each other again. At the reception, sponsored by the Irish consulate, following the reading, we renewed our acquaintance, and I promised to send Paul a copy of my journey book. He inscribed his book for us, and left us with a riddle scrawled across the title page, "What is it that a donkey sees in a tree?"

The last painting that Paul reflects upon in his book is "Grief" by Jack B. Yeats. I too am fond of the Yeats painting, having sat before it for some time at the National Gallery. (Over my desk at home I have placed a handcolored lithograph by Yeats of the stranger entering a village in the west of Ireland.) In the poem "Grief," Paul Durcan gives us his response to the painting of the same name. A middle portion reads:

> I am an art gallery attendant
> In the National Gallery of Ireland.
> I am the man
> Who sits under "Grief"
> At the head of the Gallery
> Watching fleets of feet paddling towards me.
> If anyone asks me what "Grief" means
> I say I do not know what "Grief" means.
> That is the truth. I do not know what "Grief" means.
> I do not think anyone knows what "Grief" means.
> It is a pretty picture—that is all I know about "Grief"
> After having sat under it for twenty-five years
> And I think that is all anybody knows about "Grief."

We parted as the bottles of Bushmill's and Bailey's Irish Cream were being placed on the reception table. It was good fortune meeting again on our travels, east and west. I told Paul that we think of him often on these shores—and on the prairie. I promised to work on the Donkey koan.

Wednesday, November 6, 8:30 P.M.

The maple tree in the front yard will not let its last leaves go. The wind blows this cold night; and in my house the tree makes no sound. I wait to rake the yard, snow and ice now mixed with the matted leaves of other trees. Another year I have lived in this house in town.

With the lingering maple leaves, there is a sense of the passing of a season. Not just one of the earthly seasons—spring, summer, autumn, winter—but a season of the inner life. And a stirring, as well, of something new about to begin. I sense it, but not yet seeing it, not living it daily, have nothing certain to report. I will continue my journey near home.

"Thank Heaven," Thoreau writes in the conclusion of *Walden*, "here is not all the world." "The universe is wider than our views of it," he adds. Life in this everyday world is to be informed by a view that transcends my house in town. Yet it is within this house that I awaken to the day. The journey is in the awakening. Thoreau ends his solitary tale: "Only that day dawns to which we are awake. There is more day to dawn. The sun is but a morning star." I happily await the new day.

The days are cold and snow is hard on the ground. There may be times when a wandering walk uptown will be welcomed. But most times outdoors are a hurtling against the wind on the way to a class across the river. Much like Rat in Kenneth Grahame's *Wind in the Willows*, "messing about in boats," and remarking: "In or out of 'em, it doesn't matter. Nothing seems really to matter, that's the charm of it." This morning I will listen to Herbert von Karajan's recording of "Solveig's Song" one more time. And, before lunch, there is John Prine's "Jesus the Missing Years" to be played.

For several weeks, a line that is repeated throughout Ecclesiastes has defined my days. I am drawn to this line with some urgency. Perhaps, as in Zen, the teacher appears when the student is ready. The line from Ecclesiastes reverberates in my

Metro, St. Michel, Paris

Hotel Résidence Orsay

Jardin Des Plantes

Backyard, 345 Rolfe Road

Pleasant Street, East of DeKalb

Hopkins Park Swimming Pool

Lincoln Highway, Downtown DeKalb

Merritt Prairie, Keslinger Road

Corner of South Seventh Street and East Lincoln Highway

Hollyhock, 345 Rolfe Road

Tracks of the Illinois Central Gulf Railroad at Cherry Valley Road

Mulford Road, Near Rockford

Walworth County Fair, Elkhorn, Wisconsin

Evening Stage Show, Walworth County Fair

Bookshelf in the Livingroom at Home

Pleasant Street

Reading Room, DeKalb Public Library

# Part IV

# Once My Father Traveled West to California

I had not known of its existence. It was the very first photograph of the trip, taken by Alice just as my father and Mervin were about to begin their journey. In the driveway of the Kittleson farm, Mervin and my father stand beside the Model T. Luggage is strapped to the running board. Mervin has placed his cap on the radiator and strikes a pose. Both are dressed in their traveling suits. Alice kindly gave me the photograph, and I have made a copy for you to see.

They were now on the road. Leaving early Monday morning, September 16, 1924. They drove southwest to Beloit, down to Rockford, along the Rock River to Dixon, and then onto the Lincoln Highway that would take them all the way west. The adventure of a lifetime had begun.

Reaching Clinton, Iowa, that evening, they were 120 miles from home. The first lines home were written that evening on a post card to Aunt Kate: *Arrived here at Clinton, Iowa at six o'clock. Are spending the night at the tourist camp. Have just gone over the Mississippi River. Had three flat tires, but didn't have to buy any new ones.* Signed *Floyd.*

Certainly Aunt Kate would be the first person my father would write to on the trip. Kate, his father's older sister, had taken over some of the duties after my father's mother died, when my father was five. My grandfather never married after Hattie's death, telling my father, "I would never find another woman who would be as good to my children as Hattie was." Kate worked as a dressmaker and seamstress in the homes of the rich in Chicago. She had lived for periods of her life in their houses and apartments. She never married. Kate would have been sixty-nine when my father left for California. Years later, on an April night in 1942, my father came up from the house at the old place and told us that Kate was dying. Shortly afterward, the old house was torn down. For the rest of his life, my father lamented the loss of Kate's button box. Lilac bushes from long ago continue to grow around the crumbling foundation.

My father writes to Kate after two more days on the road. From North Bend, Nebraska, a few miles west of Omaha: *Camped last night at Council Bluffs, Iowa. Crossed the river into Omaha,*

Traveling on Lincoln Highway. *Railroad and dirt road in Nebraska.*

*Nebraska this morning. Have driven 64 miles this morning. Most all pavement since we got to Omaha. Have had fine weather so far. Iowa roads were real rough and hilly.* On a post card written the same day to Marjorie, he notes that *we seem to be crossing railroad tracks all the time. The trains go past us but don't have time to wait for us.*

Today Lincoln Highway continues to take the traveler west. It runs through the middle of this Illinois prairie town where I now live. Each day I cross the busy highway, DeKalb's main street, to get the morning newspaper, to go to the bookstore, or to make a doctor's appointment. Travel east or west in this country on U.S. 38, 30, or on Interstate 80 and you are likely to be on or alongside the old Lincoln Highway. I followed the route from DeKalb to Kearney, Nebraska, on a speaking tour not long ago. You can travel on Lincoln Highway 3,300 miles from Times Square in New York City to Lincoln Park in San Francisco. The highway was built to transport us to other places.

A highway crossing the continent was first proposed in 1912. Once the route was decided upon, after great deliberation among promoters of the automobile, portions of the road began to be surfaced. The first seedling mile was completed near DeKalb in the fall of 1914. Until the great popularity of auto touring in the 1920s, travel over the highway was a pioneering experience. How the highway became an integral part of American culture—an automobile culture—is well documented in Drake Hokanson's book *The Lincoln Highway: Main Street Across America*. Enough to note here that my father and Mervin, reaching Lincoln Highway in their Model T on a September day in 1924, were riding the crest of the great tour west. Road maps, guide books, filling stations, tourist camps, and miles of unpaved roads, all these were part of the new life on the road.

On the fifth day of travel, after leaving Omaha, my father and Mervin had reached Laramie, Wyoming. It was Saturday night, and my father writes to his sister Marjorie. *Camped at Cheyenne, Wyoming last night. Froze ice in front of our car. Cool here all day. Went to the Methodist church this morning and then Mervin drove 53 miles here to Laramie. We had a hamburger sandwich in Cheyenne and they were only half done. Mine made me sick to my stomach. Never was so sick in my life. Fed the fish all of the 53 miles. Was so weak just couldn't sit up. Mervin went to the store and got some oranges for me and my appetite came right back.* But they have had *no tire or car trouble in the last three days*. And my father's hayfever left him back in Nebraska. *Am feeling fine now.*

Marjorie was twenty-nine when my father started on the trip. She would live only eleven more years, dying of a ruptured appendix in 1935. I have a snapshot of her standing in a long dress in back of the house at the old place. A fur stole is draped around her shoulders, over a checkered coat. She is wearing a fine hat. And she is beautiful.

For most of her life, Marjorie worked with Kate, tending the homes of wealthy families in Chicago. In the summertime, she worked in the houses and cottages of the same families who vacationed around Delavan Lake. Many years later, long after her death, my father revealed to me, reluctantly, that she had owned and operated a tavern a few miles southwest of Delavan on Highway 14 during the last years of her life. Wherever I have lived, I have kept a framed photograph of Marjorie on my desk.

Laramie, Wyoming. *Lots of tourists at the tourist camps. About 15 cars here tonight. We use our pillows twenty-four hours each day. Sleep on them at night. Sit on them all day.*

Over the years I have tried to learn more about Marjorie. I have talked to aging neighbors who knew her. Once I found the house of the man she had dated for some years, a house I had identified in a photograph from her black photo album. The present owners invited me in and guided me through the house. Marjorie's friend, Lloyd Latta, had operated an auto repair shop back of the house. I was told that his sister Ruby had married a doctor and lived in the big house at the far end of the street. I knocked at the door, and there was no answer. Another day I will try again. Driving back on Highway 14, I passed what once was the tavern Marjorie owned and operated. Now converted to a strip and dance establishment.

My inquiries have had a singular result:

Q: "Did you know Marjorie?"
A: "Yes, I knew her well."
Q: "What was she like, her personality, her life?"

A long silence inevitably follows. Then a fading line about not knowing her that well. I suspect that Marjorie was an independent woman in her time. Not choosing to be a farmwife, a teacher, or a secretary. She followed her Aunt Kate's fashions of dress. The styles of Chicago's society women—the women Kate served as seamstress and dressmaker—set the standard. And for a woman to own and run a tavern in the 1930s must have raised eyebrows and brought censure. Marjorie was living as many women no doubt wished to live, and she paid the price for being different. To this day, the punishment of silence—to have it said that Marjorie did not exist.

The ghost in my life that I try to keep alive. One of my first investigations upon returning to the Midwest was to search through Marjorie's probate records at the Walworth County Courthouse. At the time of her death, Marjorie had about $400 in savings accounts and a 1930 Ford coupe valued at $30. She had half interest in the tavern on Highway 14, located ten miles from the farm. Included in the inventory of stock were the bottles of liquor, tobacco and cigarettes, candy and nuts, glassware, the bar and four stools, two tables and six chairs, a radio, the cabin in back of the tavern, three beds and accompanying springs. Her appendix had burst on an October day, and she had been rushed to the hospital in Beloit. My father chose to tell me little. And he missed Marjorie for the rest of his life.

On the road west, the terrain had changed abruptly since leaving Cheyenne. Gone were the gently rolling plains of eastern Wyoming, and the ascent of the mountains had begun. The highest elevation on Lincoln Highway would be reached at Sherman Summit, an elevation of 8,835 feet above sea level. The continental divide would be crossed midway in the state. My father continued his Laramie letter to Marjorie with a description of the last day-and-a-half of travel. *All one sees is hills on both sides covered with big boulders ready to roll down any minute. And some pine trees. Quite a lot of snow also.* But, fortunately, *have had no tire or car trouble in the last three days.* The cost of gasoline has risen from 13.9 cents a gallon to 20 cents with reports of 30 cents a little farther on.

He concludes the letter to Marjorie. *We meet cars from every state on the Lincoln Highway. Only a couple from Wisconsin. Lots of tourists at the tourist camps. About 15 cars here tonight. We use our pillows twenty-four hours each day. Sleep on them at night. Sit on them all day. We intend to get to Salt Lake City in about three days but you won't have time to write us there. And we don't know which trail we will take from there. But in case of sickness or anything like that a telegram would find us at the tourist camp. Had a chance to get a job with a threshing gang. Will close and make our bed. As ever your brother.*

Two days later, across the continental divide at Rock Springs, my father posts a card to Kate. *We have been traveling through mountains and deserts for the last day and a half. Haven't seen any trees or green grass in that time. Just sand and rocks. Just had fine dinner here for 35 cents.* The trip thus far—1400 miles—has cost him only $20, expenses being split between the two of them. *Fine weather here. Good thing as the roads are just dirt roads.*

They reach Green River, Wyoming. My father takes a photograph of the butte at the turn of the road. Sending the photograph home, he writes: *This is the first town we came to with green trees after spending six days on the desert. Sure looks nice. Was named Green River.*

Two more cards are sent to Kate before the travelers reach San Francisco. The salt flats and the uninhabited dry desert beyond Salt Lake City have been crossed. In search of better terrain, they decide upon a southern route that will take them down into the middle of Nevada. To Tonopah and Mina—on what is now U.S. 95—and then up to Carson City. My father writes that they have been two days crossing the desert. The roads are awful. *Just one big hollow after another in the road and dry and dusty.* He is writing from a bunkhouse on a ranch forty miles from any town. The next morning, as they are leaving, my father takes a photograph of *Mervin eating a pear near the bunkhouse where we stayed all night.*

The next night, now in Mina, my father reports that they are still traveling on bad roads in the mountains and desert. *Broke a spring on the car yesterday but got to town all right and bought a new one and put it in ourselves this forenoon. Every little ways we see wild horse or mustangs near the mountains. See quite a lot of turkeys. One flock of about one hundred.* They have traveled, by their calculations, 2,117 miles. *Only 460 miles to San Francisco.*

Up to Carson City, over the high Sierra Nevadas, through the Donner Pass, and down into the valley around Sacramento. Then on to Oakland and a ferry ride across the bay to San Francisco. Extreme changes in landscape and climate certainly were encountered. Nothing is reported on these last miles of the trip west. The travelers were relieved and thankful to have successfully made the long trip from Wisconsin to California. They had been on the road for eighteen days. And they were excited, I am sure, and filled with anticipation of what the next months in California might hold for them.

Growing up on the farm in southern Wisconsin, I sensed that we had been on the edge for a long time. Irish Catholic immigrants, now lapsed from the faith, in a farming community of Norwegians and Germans. Eyes turned toward the city, Chicago.

Green River, Wyoming. *You will notice the large boulder on top of the mountain. Looked ready to roll down on the town anytime.*

Nevada, between Ely and Tonopah. *This is a bunk house on a ranch where we stayed all night. Forty miles from one town and 160 from the next. It was built out of squares of stone and thatched roof covered with mud.*

Lincoln Highway, Nevada. *We have been two days crossing the desert and awful roads. Just one big hollow after another and dirty and dusty.*

For generations, a removal that comes with a living on the border of a strange land. A loosening of the communal bond, but a release to the world. This is the home country to which I returned after years of traveling from one place to another. Living here and there. On a road that finally leads to home.

The ethnographer had escaped for years the life of the past, the pains as well as the joys. Returning to the farm a decade after the death of his father, he felt the past impinging on the present. He had grown up on a farm, and he knew that he could never leave it completely. His education in the rural schools of the 1940s continued to provide him with values and ideals. In all that he had learned in his years of travel, in all that he had accomplished in his lifetime, growing up on the farm most surely gave him his identity. As time passed, he had found himself drawn to the land of his birth. More than ever, he felt himself a part of the natural landscape of the place. He would be remembered in the earth.

His flight from the home place thirty-five years ago had been to affirm life in a larger world. A world larger than the one circumscribed by a small farm in the Midwest. He, this ethnographer of today, traveled to know what the world might hold. But in the travel lay the contradiction and the tension: uprooted, now in need of a home. The father, no longer there, became central to the return.

When I was young, my father's age was easy to remember. Born in 1900, he was always the age of the new year. His birthday came in March as the Wisconsin winter was beginning to show signs of breaking. Farming all his life on the old place, he gradually added acres until the farm reached 160 acres. He left Dunham School after completing the eighth grade, and he did not go on to high school in Delavan. His father needed him on the farm. He also worked for a time as a weaver in the Delavan knitting mills. There he learned the knitter's knot, tied so tightly that it could pass through the needle of a machine. Years later, with great pride, he taught me the knitter's knot. He also took on a milk route that would last for years, hauling cans of milk to the Bowman Dairy in Delavan. He hauled milk first with a team of horses, then with a platform truck in the 1930s.

When growing up on the farm, I heard neighbors' tales of my father's youth and good times. He had owned one of the first Model Ts in Sugar Creek township. Growing weary of the sporting life, he settled into farming after a near-fatal skid on his Indian motorcycle on the gravel road near the farm. It was after the fall harvest of 1924 that he and Mervin Kittleson set *you for remembering me.* From a girlfriend in Delavan he receives a box of six handkerchiefs, three white ones and three with colored edges, initialed. Kate goes to South Dakota to be with her brother Tom who dies at the end of the month. Christmas day my father and Mervin are invited to dinner at the Fredricksons'. *Had a good time and a dandy turkey dinner with all that goes with it.* They play pool and go to church. On December 28th my father reports the highest tide of the year with the water coming up to their cottage door.

The new year arrives and seals come up on the beach near the cottage. My father kids Marjorie that *maybe you would like a seal skin coat. If so I'll catch you a couple. ha ha.* They continue to work from 7:30 in the morning to 4:30 in the afternoon, with a half hour for lunch, and on Saturdays they quit at one o'clock. They have received a box of homemade fudge from a friend of Mervin's. They have gone to a show titled "What Shall I Do," starring Dorothy Mackaill. Plans are being made for a trip to Catalina Island. And my father is beginning to think about buying a suitcase for when they will have to pack and return home. *The old one is pretty well shot.*

*Stayed at Long Beach all afternoon. Went to a band concert at the auditorium and to a show and vaudeville.*

The February days are getting longer. *Sun rises a few minutes earlier and sets later every night. Real foggy.* Oil is gushing 100 feet from a well two miles from the cottage. *Some sight.* Shows and vaudeville at Long Beach, and *a glass show where a man made everything you could think of out of glass.* A fish dinner, *best I have ever eaten, all for 30 cents.* My father asks Kate, *What does pa want to buy another horse for? Has too many now to farm with.* He notices all of the auctions and the selling of farms in a copy of The Delavan Republic which Kate has sent to him. *Will surely be a lot of moving around home this spring.*

The last week of February my father writes to Marjorie to tell her about the trip to Catalina Island on Sunday. From the boat *Avalon* he took pictures, *and if they are good will send some home. There were over 500 passengers on the boat. About ten got seasick and fed the fish. Saw a whale come to the top and gush water in the air three times then disappeared. After we reached Catalina*

*Yesterday we went to Long Beach to church. Stayed at Long Beach all afternoon. Believe I told you all about the amusements there.*

*Island we took a ride on the glass bottom boat. Just wonderful to see animal and plant life in the ocean. Could look down in the water to the depth of 75 feet seeing the different kinds of fish, clams and weeds. One sea weed that grows to the surface of the water that potash and iodine are made from called Kelp was real interesting.*

On Catalina Island, William Wrigley's mansion is seen from a distance high on the side of the mountain. *Mervin and I thought that we have helped him build it by chewing so much of his gum. Then—each of us bought a souvenir, an abalone shell. Has all the different colors of the rainbow.* Among the packet of letters found on the porch last summer is the *circular that I will send with this letter*, a circular titled boldly EXCURSION DELUXE TO CATALINA—THE MEMORY LINGERS.

The letter of March 2nd to Marjorie begins: *Received your letter today and as dad says to come home will work until March 11th. Then they will go to Riverside to visit a minister who used to live in Millard*—*Mrs. Kittleson said to be sure to go there*—*and take a week or more to go to San Diego and Tijuana. So won't get home until about March 25th. The days are hot, in the 80s, and the beaches are covered with bathers. Store windows are full of spring hats and everybody says "spring is surely here."* At home, *is the feed holding out?*

The last letter from California—written to Kate—is dated March 9, 1925, Seal Beach, California. *We went to Los Angeles Saturday afternoon. Went to the depots to find out about train times, fares and so forth. Think that I will come home on the Southern Pacific for anything that I know of now. I will leave Los Angeles Monday, March 23rd at ten o'clock a.m. and get to Chicago at seven o'clock a.m. Thursday March 26th, and will probably get to Delavan on the one o'clock, Thursday March 26th.* While at the depot he took note of whether travelers were using bags or suitcases. *There were ten suitcases to every one bag being used. Suppose its because most of the people were traveling a long ways and had lots of clothes that a traveling bag wouldn't hold. Thus: I bought a black genuine cowhide suitcase and it won't be a bit too big for all I have to put in it. The fare home will be about $105.00.* Mervin will be taking the train to Spokane, Washington to

*Sunday went to Catalina Island. Was a dandy trip. Went on the boat* Avalon. *Took some pictures. If they are good will send some home. There were over 500 passengers on the boat.*

KJ's Tap on South Fifth Street and East Lincoln Highway

Sullivan's Tavern, East Lincoln Highway

Change, all is change, nothing remains the same. Not long ago, we went to the basement to get relief from the sweltering heat of the afternoon. At night we slept there to get some relief from the noise of the speeding trains loaded with the summer harvest. This morning, bundled in wool, I make a few notes while listening to Beethoven's last symphony, number nine in D minor. I listen, as well, to the songs of Lou Reed and John Cale in memory of Andy Warhol. With a little more sun, later in the morning, I will drive to the lumber yard. On my way, I hope to photograph the tracks along the abandoned passenger station.

Perhaps it is because of the impermanence of all things that we value life so dearly. And in accepting impermanence, we lessen the suffering that comes in holding on to that which cannot be saved. All things decay and change to something else, this body and self included. What is there to cling to, to be nostalgic about, when we but die to another life?

We see, we look for a sign, but in the end our trust goes beyond what can be seen. Call it imagination and a faith by which we live. A soliloquy, about the delight of swimming, delivered in Brian Friel's new play *Molly Sweeney*, has these lines: "Just offering yourself to the experience—every pore open and eager for the world of pure sensation, of sensation alone—sensation that could not have been enhanced by sight—experience that existed only by touch and feel, and moving swiftly and rhythmically through that enfolding world; and the sense of such assurance, such liberation, such concordance with it." We live daily in this town—as in all towns—with something like a faith in what cannot fully be seen. Still, I photograph with a passion. A way of knowing by not knowing, of being here intently.

The epistemology of our time is in the attention we give to the world of appearance. In the Western world, we have dwelled in Plato's cave, between the fire and the wall, watching the shadows dance. But always the yearning for a clearer vision of the thing itself. To be enlightened in some manner. The sacred text (I Corinthians 13: 12) reads:

> For now we see though a glass, darkly;
> but then face to face:
> now I know in part;
> but then shall I know even as also
> I am known.

In the meantime, there is the wonder of our daily existence. W.H. Auden's words speak to us in town this cold, after the holiday, morning:

> In the meantime
> There are bills to be paid, machines to keep in repair,
> Irregular verbs to learn, the Time Being to redeem
> From insignificance.

Through our imaginations and our daily observations, in the meantime, we give a semblance of order to what we experience as life. And in so doing, find beauty in the world, in this town. Stephen Sondheim, in his musical *Sunday in the Park with George*, writes the line, "What the eye arranges/Is what is beautiful." We make order out of chaos.

On that other level of reality, however, that level of the ultimate and the absolute, everything is simply as it is. All is perfect: the earth turns, the seasons come and go, the tides rise and fall. But we sentient beings exist on the relative plane. A world of right and wrong, war and peace, birth and death. We may at times, with some enlightenment, sense the emptiness (the fullness and the oneness) of the ultimate and the absolute. Being human—in body, mind, and heart—we must necessarily give our attention to the relative problems of our existence. The moral questions, however relative they may be, are the questions by which we live daily. Yet, we live in two worlds, the absolute and the relative. Such is the problem of being human.

This day on my way home from the tracks I invoke the Sanskrit word *tathata*. An incantation to the ultimate and the absolute. The "suchness" of reality: everything is as it is, beyond the knowing mind. Reality-in-itself. In the darkening afternoon, I entertain beyond human experience the notion that nothing is born and nothing is dying. Birth and death exist only on the relative plane.

At home I read the words of Thich Nhat Hanh on the waves in the water. "Observing the ocean, we see that the waves are always there being born and being destroyed. A wave seems to have a beginning and an end. But waves are also water. If a wave is capable of seeing itself as water, it transcends all beginnings and all endings. As far as the waves are concerned, there may be birth and death, but as far as the water is concerned, no birth and no death can be found anywhere. Only if the wave realizes that it is water can it be emancipated from birth and death. When you look into the nature of interbeing, when you know that you are that nature of interbeing, you will be free."

What appears to be film noir—DeKalb noir—in my daily human existence is simply emptiness, or suchness, in the realm of the absolute. I may die to the day (I *will* die to the day), but in larger perspective there will be no death. I know this in moments of awareness, but still there will be the chill in my spine when the train from the west passes through town tonight and sounds its lonely whistle.

☙

I hope to photograph the moving train as it passes through town. My attempts up to now have come to naught. Three or four freight trains speed through DeKalb every hour, twenty-four hours a day. But when I wait with the camera on the tripod, no trains appear. I am beginning to sense what it was like for Peter Matthiessen climbing the Himalayas, hoping to sight the snow leopard. Finally, as in all journeys, it is the search itself that is important.

At home, at the place I now call home, the whistle can be heard again. A nineteenth-century technology—the train and the whistle. A blasting of the whistle once removed cattle from the right-of-way granted the railroads. Today, a century and a half later, the whistle ceases to serve public safety. Accidents at the crossings and suicides along the tracks are recorded each year in town. I have written to the local newspapers protesting the noise of the train and the ineffectiveness of the whistle. In letters to the editor, I have proposed that the tracks bypass town in the same way that the interstate highway diverts car and truck traffic. Letters from fellow citizens, in response to my letters, suggest a nostalgia for trains. Anyone bothered by trains, I am told, can leave town. I think that I am learning to live with trains, as I watch and wait and listen.

Earlier this year, a colleague in the history department observed how our minds reside in disciplines with regional, national, international, and sometimes cosmic, dimensions. Yet, we live daily as citizens, as responsible human beings, here in town. Our bodies and emotions are attached to this place, but only portions of our minds dwell here. Much of the time we are not "here" at all. We make our accommodations, our adjustments; and for me, the events of the here and now—in this Midwest town—are the substance of my intellectual work. The local and global become one and the same. Not just this train in this town, but *the* train—as fact and metaphor—in this turn-of-the-century existence.

Is it not, then, essentially a question of being at home? Our human impulse is to feel at home, to be at one with a place, a place that finally may be the whole of the universe. And it is with some sense of home, of belonging to a place, that we humans have, as Stanley Cavell has noted, "the promise and power of leaving it." With home, we have the possibility of leaving home, of distancing ourselves from the familiar, of wandering into a larger world. Thoreau, in building a cabin in the woods near Concord, was free to travel a whole world. Each day we leave home. As a wanderer, in thought and spirit as well as in space, I leave town.

We are firmly within a philosophical tradition, whether of the East or the West. Friedrich Nietzsche, as a European, wrote: "If you would like to see our European morality for once as it looks from a distance, and if one would like to measure it against other moralities, past and future, then one has to proceed as a wanderer who wants to know how high the towers in a town are: he *leaves* the town." And whether the objective is to compare or simply to live, the wandering monk leaves home and enters the marketplace—with helping hands. There is a world for the caring. Leaving home, for whatever duration, is an act of discovery, an act of being human in relation to all others. This is our true dwelling. Between ages—between modern and postmodern—we travel widely.

Still, I know that I never will be fully at home in this town or in this world. We ultimately are of some other place; we are born to this world, and we leave it. In the meantime, we search for home and, simultaneously, we long to distance ourselves from it. Such is our human condition.

Yesterday, after a snowfall during the night, I set up my camera at Seventh Street to photograph the tracks. Without expectation, without thought or hope, what do you suppose happened? A train from the west roared toward me, and I quickly pushed the shutter release. The camera on the tripod was overturned by the force of the passing train. Recovering the camera in the snow, I hoped that I had captured on film the image of the train. Snow blew in the wind as the train sped out of town toward Chicago.

For some time, I have been reading Robert Burton's *The Anatomy of Melancholy*, that seventeenth-century book that continued to be revised until the author's death in 1640. The writing—and the immense reading upon which the writing is based—was Burton's life. Reading and writing were for Burton life itself.

I read *The Anatomy of Melancholy* for the same reasons today that Burton wrote the book three and half centuries ago. To keep busy and to occupy this gift of the human mind. The paradox of such labor, however: In distracting myself from the ultimate meaning of existence, I raise questions that lead me only further into the abyss.

Winter Storage, Virgil Cook & Son, East Lincoln Highway

Gas Pump at the Auto Repair Shop, Back of East Lincoln Highway

Railroad Tracks and Coal Chute, East End of DeKalb

Chicago & North Western Railroad, Downtown DeKalb

Burton's book may be known best as a vast dissertation on the psychological state known as melancholy. It is certainly that, a book filled with the immense learning of the past, but it is also (if not primarily) a document of one person attempting to master the proliferation of learning available in published form. The invention of the printing press a century and a half before Burton's time made scholarship readily accessible, and made reading an occupation in itself. Melancholy, sometime a morbid sadness, was a mental state many claimed to suffer in Burton's century.

The melancholy that concerned and afflicted Burton is the mental and psychological condition that comes with the search for knowledge. The more Burton read about melancholy, the more he tried to know the meaning of melancholy, the more he experienced melancholy. And is this not our condition today as intellectuals? The more we seek to know, the more we devise methods of investigation, the more depressed in mind and spirit we become.

Yet we continue to seek the holy grail of knowledge. I enter the local bookstore to place another order for a book that I have seen reviewed or cited in something I have read. Perhaps one more book will provide me with the answer (the answer to what?), or one more reading will set me on the right course. I enter the bookstore as if entering a temple, a sanctuary, a sacred place. There is ever the hope of salvation, of finding myself in the word. My bookcases at home are filled with books yet to be read. This winter I have built two more bookcases to hold the overflow.

More snow fell during the night. Rather than shovel the driveway, I will stay indoors and read. Carefully working the mind, I turn to insights beyond the Western tradition. I read again the lines of Chuang Tzu:

> If you persist in reasoning
> About what cannot be understood,
> You will be destroyed
> By the very thing you seek.

132  FOR THE TIME BEING

Keep it simple today. I will not worry, or speculate about, the missing mass in the universe that is reported in the morning newspaper. The earthquake on the other side of the planet is enough for one day. The distant whistle of the train brings me to attention. Loneliness is only a thought. And so is the abyss.

※

The abiding passion for Robert Burton—lasting a lifetime—was melancholy. Mine has been the search for reality. What is real, and how can reality be known? How Platonic the questions are, in thought and belief. An order is assumed, an order of "forms" (or "ideas") that transcends observation and experience, a higher realm, preexistent and eternal. We assume that the human mind, in all its reason, can apprehend a world beyond things physical.

Such is the Western belief system: there is a reality beyond our everyday experience, and this reality can be known by the human mind. That there is more to existence than appearance, that there is an essence beyond our own sense experience. A Western religion, the belief in something that is beyond this world, an eternal unknown, sometimes called God. We are mystics, then, in our spiritual and intellectual lives. We hope to see beyond the shadows of the cave.

Nonetheless. This wintering spirit—*spirit noir*—seeks no reality outside of the experience of each day, and each night of passing trains. I know only what is sensed in this moment. A walk downtown in the snow, an hour at my desk, a whistle in the distance. The wonder of this existence.

A mind that now cannot know of the existence of anything beyond experience. A mind—limited by its own evolutionary capacity. This grand piano of a mind which provides the space for the music (our thoughts) to be played in. We humans cannot step outside of our existence; we cannot know if there is anything outside of the grand piano. And we do not know if our existence is other than a dream. A dark night of the mind.

It is not for us to know what cannot be known. To seek such knowledge is beyond our capacity as human beings. The simple teaching of Buddhism wisely informs us: "Only don't know." We have the mind to ask questions of reality, existential and ultimate, but we do not have the capacity to answer the questions. Such is our human condition, as Albert Camus said, a condition of the absurd. Humility, mixed with wonder, makes more sense than the continuous pursuit of knowing what cannot be known.

We stand before the mystery of existence. Our humanity is in the recognition of our common inability to know for certain. Our fate, and our saving grace, is to be compassionate human beings. Whatever we attempt to know is known in love. Not in manipulation and control, not in the advancement of a separate self, but in the care for one another. This is reality enough.

In the wisdom of the East, the other word for reality is *enlightenment*. A realm of neither knowing nor not knowing. Neither existence nor nonexistence. Dōgen, the thirteenth-century founder of Soto Zen, writes: "This realm of reality is also called enlightenment, and it is also called the inconceivable realm. It is also called wisdom and it is also called not being born and not passing away. Thus all phenomena are not other than the realm of reality; hearing of this nonduality and nondifference, do not give rise to doubt." A place where there is nothing on which to dwell. A silent realm of reality, known (and unknown) in moments of enlightenment.

There is no distinction to be made between the experience of this world and transcendent meaning. Appearance, in the fullness (or emptiness) of awareness in the here and now, is all the meaning in the world. With enlightenment, there is nothing that has to be done.

Only with the dropping off of the self is the nature of all things revealed. Because, as Francis Cook writes in a commentary on Dōgen, "reality is nothing but that which we encounter in the absence of the craving, fear, sentimentality, prejudice, discrimination, and judgment that originates in the small self." In other words, reality is experienced when the self (the egoself) is lost. Then we are enlightened and opened to the reality. An enlightenment that is more than mere satisfaction about the nature of reality; an enlightenment that liberates this human being. A freedom to be at one with the world.

Lives, then, are lived spontaneously without the weight of concern regarding consequences for oneself. "For this reason, compassion is a very simple matter; one forgets the self and does what is needed," Cook writes. We have thus moved from the search for reality—the craving for reality—to the living of a compassionate life. A compassionate life lived by simply acting in accord with awareness of our oneness with all others and with all things—beyond self, beyond the knowing self. The end is compassion, and the elimination of suffering, rather than knowing reality. Without effort, reality is fully experienced.

"So the point is," Alan Watts notes in his book *The Way of Liberation*, "if you want life, do not cling to it, let it go." And in the phraseology of Zen Buddhism, "You cannot achieve this by thinking, you cannot achieve this by not thinking." We watch the trains go by. We watch, we photograph, we listen—this our practice for the time being.

The last roll of film from my winter of wandering is being developed. Black and white, night and day, the noise and the silence, the freezing and the melting, loneliness and companionship, life and death—each comes with the other. The lesson of ecology, the lesson of no-self, all things are interdependent and finally all things are one. May I neither dwell nor not dwell on the question of reality again. This I have learned during the winter of ninety-four/ninety-five. Near the end of a century.

## Postscript

Nearly two years have passed since I walked the streets and photographed this prairie town in a certain frame of mind and cast of spirit. The trains still speed through town with blasting horns. Physically the town looks about the same, although a few more of the stores on Lincoln highway have closed and the buildings stand vacant. I am not bothered nearly as much by the sounds of the train. My ethnography was a cure of sorts.

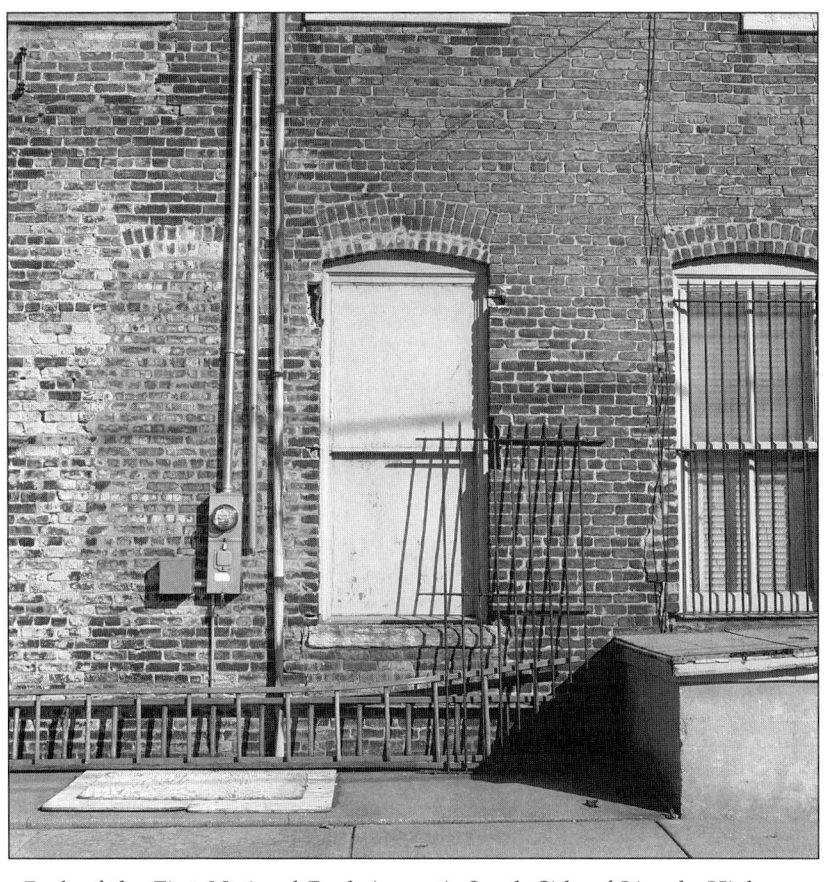

Back of the First National Bank (vacant), South Side of Lincoln Highway

Hintzsche Fertilizer, East Lincoln Highway

Demolition of the Old Post Office Building,
Corner of Fourth Street and West Lincoln Highway

Cemetery Behind the First Congregational Church, North First Street

Still, I am an ethnographer and a photographer, an observer playing with the pieces of a puzzle. But realizing now that the pieces need not fit together. Much of my time is still spent in solitude by choice and by circumstance. I live and work necessarily within this condition.

Only days ago an unnamed reviewer responded to my earlier ethnographic telling of living in this Midwest town. I was wisely counseled, and I hope to live in light of the advice offered by the reviewer. Essentially, the reviewer was concerned about the melancholy produced by the search for the meaning of human existence, and suggested that my depression was the result of following the old and now out-of-favor modernist illusion of the spectator theory of knowledge—of knowledge at a distance. Such a stance was never meant to confront metaphysical questions of the meaning of life.

Two years ago, in the project that came to me out of need, I intentionally let myself be open to the questions of existence. My position was one of being on the edge, of being vulnerable to the world. Rather than pretending to be an observer who had it all under control, I opened myself to both the wonder and the horror of existing in a vast and ultimately unknowable universe. With such an opening, various and multiple selves were allowed to exist simultaneously. I was an observer of a place, a reader of the texts of others, a photographer of abstracted black and white images, a sometime participant in one community or another, a philosopher of everyday life, and a householder. Too many voices at once, perhaps. But such is the price, or the reward, of letting things be as they may.

Likely I will soon be leaving this town. I have hopes of a new beginning, of removing myself from the old sensibility. With the move, someplace beyond this Midwest noir, I will practice the direction offered by my reviewer. That direction is a sense of knowledge that is participatory, knowledge that is aimed at empathy and caring rather than at explanation and mastery. The purpose is to know how to live compassionately. Knowledge as a practical social skill rather than as an intellectual enterprise. The emphasis, still existential, is on action—a life of participation and mutual construction, a life that may include ethnographic research as engagement. My reviewer adds, "It is not whether to dwell on reality or give it up, but rather what kind of reality one wants to fashion." It is a choice, then, of "what illusions to live life by." And so beyond this "lonely whistling."

The eternally human problem of finding a home, is it not? In his book on ethnographic fieldwork in Aboriginal Australia, Michael Jackson turns our existential attention to "being-at-home-in-the-world." Home is a lived relationship rather than an entity or essence. Knowledge is knowing how to create a home with others in the world. Our craving for objective knowledge is replaced with a desire to know how to live. "Knowledge then becomes a way of carrying us into more fruitful and caring relationships with others, rather than distancing ourselves from others in the name of objectivity." Knowledge is thus a form of worldly immanence, being with others, here and now. Instead of being alienated from the world, with intellectualist conceptions of knowledge, we are at home.

The train has taken us metaphorically home. We are moving to where we, with care, shape the course of our lives. The whistle no longer seems to be the loneliest of calls. We are in the world together.

# Part VI

# The Professor, a Portrait

east coast to talk to experts in the study of the life course. But mainly, and this was not a factor mentioned in his proposal, the professor recovered gradually from the dissolution of his marriage. The divorce of his lifetime. His own crisis, his own journey, I will say, was as much spiritual as it was anything else. With the sabbatical, with time, he would go on.

---

He would have a physical examination. The professor goes to the doctor. The immune system is failing. This he learns. We all wait for the sentence of death. It is with us all the time, and finally pronounced. "Your condition is chronic." You must live with that, Professor. With that.

---

That. The word, the idea in the word, became important to him. He read *The Bhagavad Gita*, and in it the Sanskrit words *tat tvam asi*: "Thou art that." Sri Krishna in a dialogue with Arjuna instructs: "Realize that which pervades the universe and is indestructible; no power can affect this unchanging, imperishable reality." Krishna then adds: "Death is inevitable for the living; birth is inevitable for the dead. Since these are unavoidable you should not sorrow. Every creature is unmanifested at first and then attains manifestation. When its end has come, it once again becomes unmanifested. What is to lament in this?"

Becoming one with *that*. The otherwise nameless, sometimes called God. The professor is coming to a realization of his true being, his native state, his universal Self. Where death has no reach. In the *Taittiriya Upanishad,* he learns how fear might be ended.

> When one realizes the Self, in whom
> All life is one, changeless, nameless,
> formless,
> Then one fears no more. Until we realize
> The unity of life, we live in fear.

Still, the professor holds to this mortal life. He clings to the joys and sufferings of each day. Do not we all? Even knowing our true nature?

The professor takes to the road. He travels with his camera, photographing. Making a visual record; exploring; awakening to the day. Becoming one with the universe. His daily meditation.

The professor is pursuing the sublime. This is his project. The research that engages him. Experiencing a state of mind where subject and object are fused into one. He takes Percy Shelley's poetic line, written in awe of Mont Blanc, as his daily word: "All seems eternal now." At the end of the day of photographing, the professor writes in his journal: "All seems eternal when I see a landscape in the silence of the moment, when I allow myself to be struck with wonder. The eternal is known concretely when I am present, quiet, without thought of past or future, unbounded by time." He quotes a line from Wittgenstein. "If we take eternity to mean not infinite temporal duration, but timelessness, the eternal life belongs to those who live in the present."

For a year, the professor travels and photographs the landscape around this prairie town. Through all the seasons of the year. I will not describe to you the many photographs he took or quote the entries from his journal. Let it be noted simply that the travel, the photographing, and the writing held the professor's complete attention for the year. Yes, he has hopes that his explorations will someday be published for you to read and to see. To enjoy, and to help you with your own life. But in the meantime, he travels to know eternity. The road, near home, is his teacher.

The human condition of having to find meaning in the course of everyday life. In the living. All else is death. The professor, the wayward professor, the existentialist of this story, finds essence in existence.

He reads Camus's *The Stranger* another time. A new translation. Meursault is waiting to be executed. He at last speaks of the wonder of his existence: "In that night alive with signs and stars, I opened myself to the gentle indifference of the world." Nearing death, Meursault knows life. And the gentle indifference of the world. Again the professor reads Camus.

Let us pause here briefly. It has occurred to me, and likely you have noted this, that the professor who thinks he knows so little—the unknowing one—appears to be firmly attached to at least two assumptions. And does it not appear, at first glance, that the assumptions are in some contradiction? I am referring, on the one hand, to his faith in the unity of life, a oneness in the universe that can be sensed in a sublime state of mind. On the other hand, in an existentialist mode, the professor holds to an indifference in the universe. That meaning is only in the present moment, in the living of each day, that there is no knowable meaning beyond the present. Perhaps he wishes us to pose his life as a contradiction, as in a Zen koan, and then resolve the difference at some other level of understanding. Or maybe he doesn't care what we think about his life; we have our own lives to live.

I would add only this. Now in our investigations. Any unity in the universe is unknowable to the human mind. Yet, to be human is to have faith in something. And perhaps the greatest faith is that of not knowing. The courage not to know. In all the wonder of this existence, the professor carries on.

The house today is filled with the soft and melancholy sounds of music. The professor is listening to the adagios from Schubert's String Quintet in C Major and Beethoven's String Quartet No. 15 in A Minor. Slow movements, the late works of each composer. Recordings sent to him recently from afar by his daughter. Outside, snow falls gently. The first snow of the season.

During the last month, the professor has been immersed in reveries of the past. To be specific, he has been thinking about his father. Last summer, he found on the porch of the farmhouse, in the faded veneer music cabinet, the letters his father had written home seventy years ago on his trip to California. His father would then have been twenty-four years old. After the fall harvest in 1924, he and a friend traveled west in the Model T Ford. They would stay in California for six months, working first in restaurants and then with a crew building towers for electric power. It was the one big trip his father would take in a lifetime. Returning in the spring, he would marry and raise a family. The letters are what remains of the writings of his father. The professor, as you can imagine, was pleased to discover the letters. In the music cabinet on the porch of the farmhouse.

The potato famine in Ireland of the 1840s had brought the professor's ancestors to this country. His great-grandparents migrated to the midwest and purchased a thirty acre homestead. The site, still called the old place, was the birthplace of the professor's father. His father stayed on the farm all his life, with the exception of the trip to California. He died twenty-five years ago, on a snowy day, near the barn.

In a gray metal box on a shelf above his desk, the professor keeps the letters his father wrote home during his months away from the farm. There are also the few letters he wrote to his son, the professor, in later years. The professor doesn't read them often. Only when he feels he is losing the sound of his father. A few letters to assure the professor of his father's existence.

―※―

I have just read the words of Cézanne: "One minute in the life of the world is going by. Paint it as it is." I, your narrator, am a witness to a life. With you, in the moment of writing, I have reverence for all that passes. This ephemeral life. A continuing report on the life of the professor. A world going by.

## 3

Not as often as he used to, a year or so ago. But still, especially on a foggy morning in fall or winter, he drives the county roads until he finds a cemetery. Today he stopped at one of the homesteader cemeteries along Annie Glidden Road. One-half acre of falling and fading tombstones, burials from a hundred years ago. A small stone marks a grave: "Our Little Eddie Sleeps." A single evergreen tree stands in the mist—an ancient symbol of everlasting life.

The professor imagines the early-nineteenth-century paintings of Caspar David Friedrich as he wanders through the cemetery. Ruins, churches, sea and mountains, trees, fog and mist, and graveyards. Gazing into the infinite distance, the professor is at home. At the edge of the world, in the realm of the timeless, near the luminous void. Words once spoken by the painter the professor later in the day writes in his journal: "I have to be alone and know that I am alone if I am to examine nature closely and experience her completely." Boundless, wholly empty, and still.

※

The professor has a new car. One that suits him well. No longer the red car. Something closer to gray, yet with a metallic luster. And he wonders. As we all do with age. Will this be my last car?

He enjoys the ride. Traveling down the road. Miles to go. The professor, the wayward one, once wrote these lines: "The road is a home place in which we may live in eternity. The journey is inward to an unknown place. Home is where I have never been before. Here, now, in this place as I travel, I am at home."

※

I want to make an entry to provide you with a piece of background information about the professor. Nothing of any detail, but a general observation relevant to the character of the professor. It has to do with the many moves he has made in his years. Constantly, it seems, packing up everything—pulling up stakes—and moving to another place. Others have commented on this at greater length.

Let me simply note that since the time of becoming the professor, of obtaining work as a university professor, he has moved innumerable times. From town to town, city to city, and from one house or apartment to another. He left the middle of the country to remove himself from a way of life, or better stated, to experience a larger world. Subsequent jobs were as much the occasion to move to another place as they were for career advancement.

He had reached New York City by his early thirties, and was by then a full professor. These were years of great excitement in his life, and from accounts that others have given, a high point in the academic and political lives of many professors. But even here, in the center of the world, there came a time to leave.

In quieter places, he would begin to identify again with the natural world. To search for the spiritual part of himself that had become lost in the material world. To realize his true nature. He was stirred by the lines of the Swedish poet Pär Lagerkvist: "Some day you will be one of those who lived long ago." There was a period of questions without answers, and then the realization that answers were unnecessary. The lines of Rainer Maria Rilke furnished sustenance. "Be patient toward all that is unresolved in your heart. Try to love the questions themselves." And finally the realization, after a few more moves, that even the questions were no longer important. The wonder and the peace of a beginner's mind. "Only don't know."

Whether to go or stay. The journey has no beginning and no end. The decision is not ours. Unborn to the world. The professor's life, in all the travel from one place to another, is something like this.

⁕

I walked uptown this morning to the public library. After the professor had returned from retreat in the monastery, he read the diary that John Howard Griffin had kept while working on a biography of Thomas Merton. Griffin was writing at Gethsemani monastery, himself in retreat, and feeling the effect of his own aging. The professor had marked a passage in Griffin's diary, and I wanted to study the passage that had gotten his attention. I thought you might be interested.

Griffin observed of himself: "I sense a perceptible diminuation of intellectual gifts. I have noticed it for some time. I do not make any great thing of it. It does not really concern me, except it is there and apparent." He attributes it to age, or perhaps the shock of illness. His vocabulary is reduced, but, at the same time, "the sense of overwhelming mysteriousness grows in me." Griffin no longer seeks intellectual understanding, nor does he readily engage in rational discourse. "The things that fill me now cannot be uttered with any accuracy, though I sometimes struggle to utter them. I find that I end up writing about concrete rather than speculative things—about the way wind stirs the leaves of a single branch of a tree." He adds: "I go along with it. I can do nothing else, and I am not at all sure this is not simply right for me at this time in my life."

No longer the passion to learn a truth. But rather, the giving of oneself to whatever is there. "To the play of sunlight on leaves, to the sound of a voice or the sound of a soul; to whatever chooses to reveal itself." Any understanding is a gift, not sought after, but appreciated when granted. The professor has read this, and he has noted it. Not long ago, he copied the passage into his journal.

⁂

High on the mantel a candle burns. Anton Bruckner's Ninth Symphony is playing. Solemn, majestic, mystical, left unfinished in Bruckner's last days. Dedicated "to our dear Lord." An elegiac farewell. In place of the unfinished finale, a recording of Arvo Pärt's *Te Deum.* "We praise thee, O God."

He, the professor, has no name for a Supreme Being. In part, because he cannot imagine a being that is supreme. Anything of an ultimate nature is unknowable, and unnameable. As with the Old Testament Moses, God appears only in the revelation that "I am who I am. My name is nameless." A name would express being, and the person who knows another's name has power over that being. So much for a dogmatic theology. What is left is mysticism. Not knowing. The professor's theology.

And is it not true, as well, that the professor of my telling remains unnamed? I too prefer mystery to knowing. Mystery to solution and to certainty. We dwell in the house of an unknowable universe. If universe it is.

For thirty years, the professor's days have been measured by the reading of the *New York Times*. There have been few days without the *Times*. When visiting friends and relatives, in whatever part of the country, and in the remotest of places, he has sought the elusive morning newspaper. He has walked railroad tracks out of the woods, driven the roughest of roads, and taken buses across town to find the *Times* of the day. Over the years, a sense of continuity.

And once the newspaper has been found, it is to the obituaries that the professor turns. Others have questioned this habit, wondering whether there is a morbid curiosity. I think not. Rather, a delight in how a life has been lived. On some days, the obituary of one he has known. In each obituary, a report of how another mortal existence has come to an end.

But not an end to life. The wayward professor is of the Eastern view: death is the opposite not of life, but of birth. What we know of life is a brief moment between two earthly events, birth and death. Life is the constant. The professor often asks his students, "Where were you before you were born?" Still, as the biologist and essayist Lewis Thomas observed, it is difficult to give up this habit of living. Thomas, age eighty, died of a long illness this week. His lengthy obituary appears in the *Times* this morning.

Also, this morning, the obituary of John Wildeman. The professor once had been his mentor. In later years they had written books together. He had come to the professor shortly after leaving the priesthood. At his university, flags have been lowered to half staff.

I assure you, the fact remains. Even with all his knowledge of Eastern philosophy, the professor fears death. His own, and the death of all others.

---

The holiday season passed. At the feast table, the professor gave his blessing: "This is Christmas, and we are here." Following the meal, still at the table, the professor delivered his lecture on the meaning of the season. In effect, the celebration of our living. Some days later, while reading an article in *The New Yorker* on the life of an autistic biologist, he exclaimed, "To be human limits the possibilities." But, then, any life is conditioned by genetics and evolution. The professor told his wife and daughter that we live, with the mice, in a grand piano. Not knowing what is beyond the bounds of our imagination. We listen to the music that is given to us.

---

When he moved into the house, he dug up and removed most of the lawn. Front and back. On the land, where there had been blue grass and fescue, he placed rocks carried from the farm, and tree stumps and logs gathered from the state park south of town. A path here and there. Then he planted perennials of all kinds. Prairie grasses and forbs. Bulbs. Spring, for several years now, brought new life around the house and in the yard, front and back.

Early this winter morning, still in the darkness of night, the professor woke up, walked down the stairs, and looked into the yard. Light from the street lamp caught the surface of the snow. The last quarter of last month's moon was high in the dark sky. A rabbit preened, cleaning the moon, and settled under the arctic willow. Dried stalks of liatrus, lilly, and sedum rose out of the snow. An old opossum walked slowly along the ridge, under the rail fence, in back. The professor watched. Each moment as the morning began and passed away.

Any thought at this time of day is simple and elementary. The basics. A few words from the Buddha: be nobody, hold on to nothing, expect nothing, identify with nothing. In Christian terms, the words of Jesus, blessed are the humble, for they shall inherit the earth. Each element of this world is instantaneously rising and dissolving. All things are interrelated, interdependent, devoid of separate existence. There is nothing of substance in this world. Nothing at all solid to hold on to. Only the mind, this human mind, makes it seem otherwise. The source of unsatisfactoriness—of our unhappiness.

We can apprehend death if we just look to the present, the birth and death of each moment. The professor has devoted his last years to such realization. Still, it comes and goes, the realization, the truth of existence. In moments of awareness—of letting go rather than having and holding on—the professor experiences happiness. Equanimity. A balance and a harmony that passes all understanding. This morning is such a morning. The weather channel is saying that a storm in the west is gathering and will sweep across the prairie by evening.

Last night on *The Simpsons,* one of the characters loudly stated, "I don't believe in nothin' no more. I'm goin' to law school." This morning, with the thermometer well below zero, the professor is saying over and over again that human life is absurd. A cruel joke, if you will. A lifetime spent creating ourselves, getting smart, working and loving, seeking security, planning for retirement. And then it is all over, obliterated, gone forever. Not even a sign given of the meaning of this existence. Oh professor, professor, stay in the moment!

You may have missed, as did the professor, the death last summer of poet William Stafford. The professor was away in New Zealand, deprived of *The New York Times* and its obituaries. The winter issue of the *Hungry Mind Review* commemorates

Stafford's life. Lines are quoted from his book *Writing the Australian Crawl*: "A writer is not so much someone who has something to say as he is someone who has found a process that will bring about new things he would not have thought of if he had not started to say them." At the writing desk each morning, some thoughts may arise.

For the record, here, I would like to enter a few lines of poetry the professor read this weekend. Pertaining to this life of writing. A gift from his daughter, John Ashbery's book of poetry *Hotel Lautréamont*. Opening lines from the first poem:

> Dear ghost, what shelter
> in the noonday crowd? I'm going to write
> an hour, then read
> what someone else has written.

We, you and I, the professor and his family, read and write to enter the world. Our creation. Our salvation. A life made in the living, in the reading and the writing.

---

Lest we get carried away with our literacy, the civilized literacy of our species, I heard Katherine Hepburn say last night in the movie video *The Lion in Winter*, "We are all jungle creatures." This just before the evening news.

---

He has been immersed in the life of the Kentucky painter Harlan Hubbard. Wendell Berry's tender account of the man and his work. Hubbard had written in his journal about a personal religion: "For myself I require a more direct revelation, not one that must come through so many minds before it reaches mine." A faith that can be seen and heard, "one that I can feel without thinking or even trying to put it into words." Still, for the painter, faith in an unknown and unknowable "mysterious spirit." Yet in the same journal entry, Hubbard ends on a note of concrete lived experience, "I bought a new axe yesterday."

The professor is wondering today about his own faith. In his journal, on occasion, he has admitted to a faith in an unnameable mystery. A life eternal that can be experienced in the moment. But today, this most winter of winter days, the professor wonders if even faith in something nameless is going too far. Is faith at all necessary? Perhaps there is only the axe to cut today's wood. A fire to keep warm by. Joy in watching the flame. Love, awe and wonder.

You have heard it said, the soul survives the death of the body. But he says unto you, it is the body that survives, and it is the soul that comes to an end. Ultimately, the energy of this mortal coil is conserved. This the professor has been professing all day long.

He is out of the house now. A walk downtown to the post office. And a stop at KJ's Tap for a beer. He will listen to stories being told of Norway.

From the vantage point of this new morning with the temperature registering twenty below zero, the professor is without a transcendent faith. No need for a faith about an existence beyond the concrete experience of the day. Just the axe, the fire, much solitude, and then a companion. The wayward professor is alive and well.

A few words to the day. This cold and beautiful day. Snow crystals in the brightness of the sun, transported by the frigid wind. Jennifer Warnes sings a Leonard Cohen song, "Came So Far For Beauty." The professor will not venture out of the house this day. He will watch and he will listen.

Solace in existential loneliness. Listening to the voices. As with Beckett, forever on our backs, in the company of voices. Dreams, songs, stories, imagination. Sometimes the invention of a God to keep us company. Thoughts. A fear now and then. Some happiness. A few words to the day.

❧

He is most himself when he is in the silence of solitude. A wind chill of minus seventy keeps the professor alone inside today. But whatever the weather of the day, he would prefer solitude. There has not been a time in his life when the words of Throeau have not applied: "I love to be alone. I have never found the companion that was so companionable as solitude." This is a solitude measured not by the presence or absence of others, but by a state of mind and spirit.

Not all that removed from the life of the wandering ascetic. A renunciation of all that is unimportant and of hindrance to a sense of oneness in the world. Life unified in simplicity. Thoreau in the woods: "It is life near the bone where it is sweetest."

For the professor, in solitude, a release from expectation and responsibility. No need to profess, to be wise, to make a judgment. Life is saved in the loss of it. In absolute love, the simplest of moments, the professor is at home.

❧

When introduced before delivering a lecture at a university in New Zealand last summer, the speaker made much of the fact that the professor still writes with a pen on a pad of paper. On parchment, the speaker said, but the professor denied this. Twenty-some books have been written by hand. The black fountain pen continues to be used. Pen and paper, the work tools.

Each morning the professor approaches the writing desk as a workman might approach the bench. As his father once worked with tools on the farm. Great satisfaction in a simple construction—a repair or a few words.

In his life, the professor has easily adapted to changes. He has been an innovator. Professing new ideas, countering conventional wisdom, readily trying on new styles of music and dress. But yet, his working style remains the same. While colleagues do their business on computers and word processors, the professor scribbles on paper with pen. Others communicate on the Internet and by e-mail. The professor has little knowledge of these forms. Avoiding even the telephone, he prefers to write letters, and wait days for a response. He savors the simplicity. He takes joy in working close to the task. With tools in hand.

Days have passed. Still snowing, with the addition of sleet. Let me bring this faith matter to some resolution before going any further. Last night the professor watched the movie video of *The Verdict* for another time. Giving special attention to Paul Newman's summation to the jury. Portraying a lawyer, restored to his calling, Newman tells members of the jury to act as if they have faith, and faith will be given. Not a call for whistling in the dark, but the courage to go on. At least this is how the professor interpreted the scene.

Faith is a trust. But a trust in what? Conventionally it is God that is the object of faith. As to that, the professor remains in doubt. But yet he goes on, trusting and accepting the wonder of this existence. And more, faith that death is but another beginning. Or better, a continuation of all that is, of all that was, and all that ever will be. A world without end. We are the stuff of stars. Of all that is the light of stars.

In the meantime, what we are given to know in this life. The living of this day. The courage to go on even as death approaches.

This morning the professor read another of the letters Rilke wrote to a young poet. He underlined the passage on faith given to the young man: "Just the wish that you may find in yourself enough patience to endure and enough simplicity to have faith." Faith that comes simply in the living. Live, and you will have faith.

As the judge would say, I will admit the following document into the record. It is a passage the professor read last night on life without God from Ingmar Bergman's book *Images*.

My parents spoke of piety, of love and of humility. I have really tried hard. But as long as there was a God in my world, I couldn't even get close to my goals. My humility was not humble enough. My love remained nonetheless far less than the love of Christ or of the saints or even my own mother's love. And my piety was forever poisoned by grave doubts. Now that God is gone, I feel that all this is mine; piety toward life, humility before my meaningless fate and love for the other children who are afraid, who are ill, who are cruel.

The professor is also reading the works of Erich Fromm. Fromm's last book, before he died in 1980, *To Have or To Be?* There was to be a sequel, a book, as Fromm described it, on "a godless religion." A study of religious experience in which the concept of god is "unnecessary and undesirable." Love in this life, Fromm had argued in an earlier book, is enough.

The kingdom is here now. God is not a person, a he or a she in another world. Nor an it. But pure creativity, the whole power of what we know as the universe, or universe of universes. How we behave toward one another is what counts. A god figure that removes us from the kingdom of this life the professor no longer seeks. Or any religious icon. As Buddhists advise: "If you meet the Buddha on the road, kill him." These days of letting go.

This morning the professor called the lawyer. Something he has been avoiding for a long time. The making of a will. For the love of others.

---

I will put this project aside for awhile. We all need a rest in this season. A time of some repose. To store up energies for another time. A suspension of activity, including our works of art. Rilke advised the young poet that "a work of art is good if it arises out of necessity." Without need, let the silence work upon us. We will return to this occupation another day. Imagine the professor happy. In silence and solitude.

## 4

A year has passed since this accounting began. A portrait started in the autumn of the year. Now the autumn of another year, September 1994. The professor has turned sixty. A life continues. Day by day. A kind of music, a life composed.

"Know this," the professor said this morning, "nothing is certain." Sounds familiar, does it not? He is in form. Life is impermanent, and that is why it is valued so dearly. And with such care. The professor has read a line this morning from an essay by Thich Nhat Hanh: "When we accept that all things are impermanent, we will not be incapacitated by suffering when things decay and die." Words for the day.

I can tell you, as with all that is impermanent, the professor has changed in the last year. There seems to be more of an acceptance of life simply as lived. This in spite of, or perhaps in relation to, the professor's renewed interest in the intellectual life. As the winter passed, and as spring and summer came and passed away, the professor gained an energy of the mind. Once again he seemed to delight in the wonders of thought. He attended several conferences, traveling twice to the west coast. He enjoyed the luxury of the Biltmore Hotel in Los Angeles. He wrote and presented papers, and his earlier writing on the meaning of social existence—and the lack of it—found receptive ears among a new generation of scholars. Whatever the reason, the professor this autumn seeks more of the life of the professor, rather than less. Still, professing that there is little to profess.

An aside. You will be interested to hear that the professor attended his high school reunion. He traveled the sixty miles north on a summer evening to be with classmates he had not seen for forty years. In fact, he was asked earlier in the summer to deliver an address to the graduates of years past. He represented those who had stayed away the many years, and he gave thanks for this time of coming together. All of us, the professor said, someday will be among those who lived a long time ago.

He spoke of the wonder of this existence. And even with such a somber message, he was reminded of the epigram that his classmates had placed beside his photograph in the yearbook. The line from Shakespeare: "Thou makest the sad heart gay."

An experimental text we have here. Not a simple realist narrative, not an objective ethnography. Mixed genres, multiple points of view, comedy and satire, subjective reflections. The stuff of a postmodern age. As author, I give you the professor. And the professor gives you me. Are we the same or different? (What is the sound of one hand clapping?) Who is to be believed? We all tell the truth.

To date, the professor noted this morning, ninety-nine percent of human existence has been spent as hunters and gatherers. Our innate sensibilities—our minds and our emotions—are an adaptation to that long-vanished environment. A wonder, then, that we humans cope today as well as we do. Hunters and gatherers in a cyberspaced world. Not unusual that often we are out of joint and a bit off balance. His mind spins. Vertigo in the right ear. An infection perhaps.

And the science section of the *New York Times* reports today of the coming apocalypse of the solar system. Life first appears on earth 3.5 billion years ago. A billion years after earth's creation. The sun passed its middle age sometime ago, and is fast moving to the final stage. A cooling that will reduce it to a white dwarf star. In the meantime, the earth will become uninhabitable to life about 1.5 billion years from today. Meaning, life on earth is nearly three-quarters over.

At his desk, the professor is experimenting with several types of ink. On five kinds of writing paper, ranging in grades of cotton parchment, and on various weights of stock. Three different fountain pens with fine, medium, and broad points. A black three-ring binder to hold the paper. He is making himself ready for the task at hand. What is an apocalypse compared to the possibilities of a blank page? You must go on.

---

Another night on the railroad. Life in this prairie town took a turn sometime last summer. Train traffic through town increased. Development to the west caused a resurgence of freight handling by rail. Seventy trains now pass through town daily. The rumbling of freight cars and the blasting of the horn rouse citizens out of their beds.

Auto accidents at the seven crossings in town continue, and in the last month two people have committed suicide in front of the speeding trains. Frightened engineers now blast the horn continuously from one end of town to the other.

The professor and his wife move in the night from one bedroom to another in an attempt to escape the noise. The professor has called the city council and he has met with the city manager. Last week his letter was published in the local newspaper. "It is time, given increased public awareness of safety and environmental quality, that the city regulates the railroad, rather than the railroad determining the life—and death—of the community." In a letter to the newspaper this week, the professor advocates a complete bypassing of the city. An interstate highway for the railroad that runs parallel to the highway that already bypasses towns across the prairie. He adds in his letter: "Blowing the horn might once have removed cattle and troublesome native Americans from the right-of-way granted the railroads, but today at the end of the 20th century, some other means would seem to be in order."

A disturbance of the peace. The professor's peace as well as that of the community. Today his nerves are rather short. As in days of old, the professor thinks seriously about moving on. A long-established tradition in the migration westward.

---

For, let us say, the last ten to fifteen years, the professor has been a mystic. Every detail of his everyday life seemed to be of consequence to his spiritual being. Life was lived in the holy. Let us assume that this stance has served him well.

Last night he told his wife that there has been a gradual change. That now he is as much sceptic as mystic. Little or nothing can be known or believed. There are no divine revelations. A simple faith only. In his journal this morning, the professor quoted the lines he had just read from Alain Danielou's memoir *The Way of the Labyrinth*. "Death is such a simple thing, a final slumber in which all the elements of our being dissolve, become inanimate matter, and return to the workshop of the gods, who fashioned us, like a broken vase that reverts to potter's clay." For the professor, some day or some night, a simple return to where he was before being born. Unborn once again.

From the high shelf of the bookcase in the basement, the professor has brought down his books on the Tao. The last months have signaled a return to the ancient wisdom. From the various translations of the *Tao Te Ching*, the professor records passages in his journal.

> Existence is beyond the power of words
> To define:
> Terms may be used
> But none of them absolute

> Before heaven and earth came forth there was something
> formless yet complete. How silent! How still! Standing
> alone and unchanging, all-pervasive and unwearying, it
> may be regarded as the mother of all things. I do not
> know its name but, if forced to give it a name,
> I would call it "TAO."

> In the pursuit of knowledge,
> every day something is added.
> In the practice of the Tao,
> every day something is dropped.

Less and less do you need to force things,
until finally you arrive at non-action.
When nothing is done,
nothing is left undone.
True mastery can be gained
by letting things go their own way.
It can't be gained by interfering.

It does not get much simpler than that. The professor has to keep reminding himself. Back to the essentials of thought and practice. Faith enough.

The professor is out photographing this morning. He is photographing inside of Sullivan's tavern. The large picture window looking out on Lincoln Highway is decorated for the holiday season. Bar stools are placed at the high table, and the television screen glows in the low morning light. He will photograph before patrons arrive for noontime sustenance.

A week or two ago, Woody Allen was interviewed on NBC's *Dateline*. He was asked at the end of the interview, "What do you have faith in?" He answered: "The power of distraction." The distractions include romance, watching a good movie, and creating something. "These distractions help you get through life." They keep you from coming face to face with questions of the meaning of existence and the ultimate fact of death. The professor makes his rounds this morning photographing in Sullivan's tavern. The power of his distraction is evident, and he practices all of his distractions with considerable deliberation this season.

Within the week, there will be the Christmas day. And on that day the professor will miss his daughters. Always a day of expectation—Christmas. Recalling the birth of the Child, and of his children. Hallelujah! His life—the professor's life—was transformed in these births. This Christmas the manger is empty. The children are gone to the world; God bless them all. Joseph and Mary are alone. They recall the nights when the stars were bright.

Each year, of late, on this day, the professor reads W.H. Auden's Christmas Oratorio. This year the words are especially welcome:

> To those who have seen
> The Child, however dimly, however incredulously,
> The Time Being is, in a sense, the most trying time of all.

It is to the present life that we must attend. The professor will read Auden's lines to his guests:

> In the meantime
> There are bills to be paid, machines to keep in repair,
> Irregular verbs to learn, The Time Being to redeem
> From insignificance.

Love, yes love, in the world of flesh. "And at your marriage all its occasions shall dance for joy."

※

Our professor has completed the writing of this winter's tale. Days of walking the snow-filled streets, photographing, and listening to the whistle of the train passing through town. A meditation on life as the century passes. The lonely whistle strikes the ear and pierces the heart in the dark of the night. A tale *noir*.

A winter skeptic. Questioning the existence of anything beyond personal experience. But even the reality of everyday life is questioned. Such thinking has put the professor in a dark mode. He has worked himself into melancholy. (The fate of Robert Burton in an earlier century.) The professor's wife suggests to him that perhaps he should try believing in something. That we cannot know if anything exists or does not exist. So why not, she tells him, believe that something exists, that there is something beyond this earthly existence, that there is meaning in the universe, that there is life after death.

All is belief—whether we believe in the existence of something or do not believe in the existence of something. The human mind cannot know anything outside of its own thinking. We are creatures of the human skull; locked in the prison of thought and belief. But, dear reader, does this not make our lives with one another ever more precious and deserving of compassion? We whirl in space toward some unknown and unknowable place among the stars.

I have been waiting for the official word before announcing to you that the professor has been granted a sabbatical leave. The word has been received, and the professor will be taking a sabbatical a year from now.

His proposal is for travel to places that will be conducive to the writing of a book on peace. Since the proposal was written, months ago, the professor has thought more about the sabbatical as being a pilgrimage. A pilgrimage—but to where and for what purpose? Perhaps a pilgrimage to find the place and the purpose. We will follow his course and note his progress.

This will be the professor's last sabbatical. He will be nearing seventy when the next sabbatical comes along. This sabbatical—this pilgrimage—likely will be the last of a lifetime.

The professor keeps posted above his desk the sabbatical proposal of a professor at another university. That professor—a professor of art—studied waterfalls along a now unused path connecting Tokyo and Kyoto. This is a model for our professor, following a path to where a work of art might be created. Pilgrimage as life's work and life's art. The end of our travel is the journey itself, a journey that need not go far beyond the door of one's own house.

Soon spring will come and summer will follow. At the moment, the professor is flying away to another country where he will deliver a lecture to an awaiting audience. His subject is of another time and another place. He will open his lecture with

Late afternoon. Mozart's Piano Concerto No. 21 in C major is playing softly on the stereo. A life of music, and a few words.

Something pulls from inside these days. I do not know what it is. I sit with this notebook before me because of feelings and thoughts unformed and unresolved. Noting this life at hand is a way of living—a way of making life possible.

An accounting seems to be in order, not so much to document this life, but to understand it in a way that will allow me to go on. To go on with some integrity, purpose, and hope. An integration of this life instead of despair. At the moment, I have a sense that I could go in either direction. Yet I travel with the hope for a happy ending. I write that I might be in a better place.

I would like to end my life knowing that it has been a good life. Maybe the accepting of this life as lived is the best I can hope for. I do not know where this investigation is going. Dear reader, we are together wherever this takes us.

---

Among the notes made at the end of an essay several months ago, I have found this: "We cannot continue this story—this life—until we give attention to what currently troubles the professor. Something more is required if we are to go on. Sadness and guilt." Sadness, melancholy, dark nights of the soul, all these are commonplace in my life. But remorse, this is something new. Certainly, in recent years, my life has been lived attentively to the moment. Without judgment, things are as they are. If I could be aware of the present, the future would take care of itself, and the past would be only a time that once was the present.

But now a good portion of my present is occupied with questions about how I have lived. Thoughts about inadequacies and wrongs, responsibilities and past conduct. At this age, into my sixties, I desire to do only what is right and what is good. And I know that I am doing the right thing when I am being good to others. This presses upon me in new ways.

A memorial service was held earlier this week for my friend and colleague, the musician Paul Steg. Several of his compositions were played in the Lutheran church on the hot and steamy Monday afternoon. A life was celebrated; kind and loving words were said. A year ago, Paul had helped me install a stereo player and speakers in my living room. We listened to the string quartets of Leos Janáček, and to Jimmy Heath's big band arrangement of "The Voice of the Saxophone." Paul had remarked on the transparent sound of the music. At the memorial service, we all remembered and gave thanks to a good life.

A morning of Haydn's symphonies. Symphonies from his great *Sturm und Drang* period, the years of storm and stress. I listen to his Symphony No. 44 in E minor. Called the "Mourning," tradition has it that Haydn wrote the adagio movement to be played at his own funeral. In a minor key, the dark message persists throughout the symphony. Music for this life.

Looking back, it is easy to see, and to lament, the worldly corruption of a life. The days, and the deeds, and the disappointments pile up. What could have been becomes evident in the hindsight of aging. In this week's issue of *The New Yorker*, John Updike reviews recent biographies of Graham Greene and makes this point. Such accounts, he concludes, "cannot convey the unearthly human innocence that attends, in the perpetual present tense of living, the self that seems the real one." Still, each of us looks back on his or her own life, and attempts an accounting. It is difficult to describe a life impartially, without judgment and lament. We create our own elegies.

Perhaps a change in paradigm accounts for the need of this inquiry. Eight years ago I began a daily journal with the inscription "A Spiritual Journey—Toward a life lived fully in the spiritual world, for an everyday life filled with the holy." I then quoted lines from a Hindu holy man: "Nothing is unattainable, my Lord, to him who enjoys your grace.... Therefore, be pleased, my Lord, to grant me unceasing Devotion, which is a source of supreme bliss." At the end of the first month, the last days of 1986, I made a telling entry:

> The driving force of this life of mine—it seems clear now—is toward a life of the holy, toward pure oneness. I am ready for the next stage in this project—to be fully immersed in the spiritual quest, best found in the monastic community—in the monastic experience—that this life will be an example of oneness in contemplation and meditation. Beyond words and concepts, much of the life is to be in silence. That I will dwell in the love of the mystery—the nameless. That I will love completely in all my life.

The journal is filled with quotations from the Christian mystics, from the Hindu sutras, from the Buddhist texts. St. John of the Cross, Thomas Merton, Bede Griffiths, *The Dhammapada*, *The Bhagavad Gita*, *The Diamond Sutra*, Alan Watts. I stayed for a week in a Trappist monastery, New Melleray Abbey, near Dubuque, Iowa. Later, I was counseled by a Franciscan priest. The following year I note: "We are *in* this world, but never *of* it. Our home lies elsewhere—beyond this world—in union with all." All of my life is to be in the realm of the spiritual.

Another story was going on at the same time. My most intimate human relationship of thirty years, my marriage, was falling apart. My response was a spiritual one, certainly a way of coping. I was not the first to turn to religion in a time of personal suffering. But, likely, the crisis in my marriage was brought about by a spiritual crisis as well.

Other journal entries were to follow. My latest journal, started in July of 1990, begins with a quote from *The Bhagavad Gita* about the eternal life. Sri Krishna is speaking to Arjuna:

> The impermanent has no reality; reality lies in the eternal. Those who have seen the boundary between these two have attained the end of all knowledge. Realize *that* which pervades the universe and is indestructible; no power can affect this unchanging, imperishable reality. The body is mortal, but he who dwells in the body is immortal and immeasurable.

Gradually, I now notice, as I read this journal, the entries become more and more attentive to the existentials of daily living. There is less devotion to what is clearly (and traditionally) the spiritual. Entries are given more to visits with my mother, letters from my two daughters, details of everyday life with my wife, and notes about our travels abroad. I note also an idea for my next book, this book now before us, a quote from a poem by W. H. Auden: "The Time Being is, in a sense, the most trying time of all." I add that my task is to find wonder in the everyday. I was becoming, once again, an existentialist.

---

Could it be that such devotion to the other world—the transcendent, the eternal—diverted me from the details (the material) of everyday life? And could it be that what gives me concern now, about living a good life, has more to do with how I live daily with others than with the state of my soul? I may be searching for some balance.

During the middle of my spiritual, mystical years, I wrote to John Wildeman, a former graduate student of mine, about matters of the spirit. I sent him one of my spiritual and autobiographical essays. He responded with a kind letter, adding these words about his own life: "Anyway, for me at this point in my own life, it seems that the deeper meanings lie not within me, but somewhere outside me. I don't matter about me anymore a whole lot. But what I do and am to others seems to me to seem to be all that counts."

I did not know it then, but John was seriously ill, and he would die five months later. Years earlier he had been a priest, and had given up the vocation to become a professor. He married and had a son. Before he died, he sent me a poem on death written by Rainer Maria Rilke two months before his own death. John also sent a poem he had written after walking the south shore of Long Island.

This life is not simple and it is not easy. Life is, the Buddha said, suffering. If I were a composer of music, I would compose a requiem for the living and the dead. Instead, I listen to the music of others, and I write words. Each life is divine in this world; each life has its own requiem.

---

The quest for the truth of life—for the truth of my life—is perhaps a search for something called salvation. An attempt to redeem this life. Things are as they are, certainly, but being human we layer the world with meaning. We seek to redeem life from insignificance; and we hope to be healed of our transgressions. This curse and blessing of the human mind. We are what we think.

Why do I tell such a sad tale? Why not simply accentuate the positive? Why do I find such affinity to the tragic. On this matter I am informed by the thoughts of my daughter Laura. She recently wrote a book on "the grimness of the truth." Laura holds that the literature most likely to be "deep," to be "true," is tragic literature. Of highest literary value, of literature the most sublime, is writing concerned with the tragic in life. The deep truths: loss, solitude, the void, the dark night of the soul, and finally death. Laura concludes a chapter with a quote from Simone Weil: "To love the truth means to endure the void, and, as a result, to accept death. Truth is on the side of death."

I write as a way of mourning. I am most at home when I am in the sublime depths of the dark void. I mourn, and I celebrate, this life and this death.

The quest for the eternal has dominated human thinking for centuries. The collapse of such questing finally took place in the nineteenth century. In retrenchment, philosophical and religious thought turned to the descriptive sciences of humankind. Comte, Marx, and Freud. But another, wholly different, response was a kind of thinking that was anti-systematic, personal, lyrical, aphoristic. Kierkegaard, Nietzsche, and Wittgenstein. Examination of one's own life—autobiography—became a legitimate way to think about the nature of everyday existence. We had become existentialists; God seemed to be dead. At least, the divine world (or any other world) was beyond the mind's ability to comprehend.

The obituary for E. M. Cioran appeared in the *New York Times* three weeks ago. I had never read the writings of this Romanian-born philosopher. Known as "the philosopher of despair," Cioran had practiced the art of the post-philosophic tradition. Cioran is quoted in the obituary as saying, "I saw that philosophy had no power to make my life more bearable. Thus I lost my belief in philosophy." He roamed the streets of Paris at night, and as he said in an interview, practiced no profession. In the night he also wrote personal essays of what it is to be human.

Late at night I have been reading Cioran's book *The Trouble With Being Born*. Aphorisms accumulate; I note some of them in my journal.

> I do nothing, granted. But I *see* the hours pass—which is better than trying to fill them.
>
> No need to elaborate *works*—merely say something that can be murmured in the ear of a drunkard or a dying man.
>
> No difference between being and non-being, if we apprehend them with the same intensity.
>
> In relation to any act of life, the mind acts as a killjoy.
>
> A book is a postponed suicide.

I have always lived with the awareness of the impossibility of living. And what has made existence endurable to me is my curiosity as to how I would get from one minute, one day, one year to the next.

The problem is not so much death as it is birth. Cioran writes: "We do not rush toward death, we flee from the catastrophe of birth, survivors struggling to forget it." The source of all suffering and infirmity, even disaster, is birth. Birth—our very existence—is the cause of death.

I returned earlier this week from a conference in Windsor, Canada. Several times during my presentation on life at the edge of the abyss (with photographs), I had to pause to catch my breath, to compose myself. It is not easy to confront the uncertainties and ambiguities of this everyday life. Yet, the wonder of Albert Camus's hero, Meursault, moments before his execution at the end of *The Stranger*. "In that night alive with signs and stars, I opened myself to the gentle indifference of the world." We go on.

---

Do you still look up into the night sky to see the planets and to watch the stars? To find Orion in the winter night, or to gaze at the full moon in July? I traveled once to the southern hemisphere to see the Southern Cross high above. A guide to many a navigator far from home.

My question is rhetorical. I do not stand in the dark night much anymore, looking into the heavens. I tend rather to open the door into the night and look for the light at the end of the street. I note the weather, and go to bed.

Things change—including this life. Nothing remains the same. There is no permanent substance to anything. Everything is in the process of becoming something else. All is impermanent.

---

Not long ago, the *New York Times* reported the discovery of a tremendous pull on the Milky Way. The unexpected discovery, we were told, may force a revision of some basic notions about the universe. We were informed: "What is tugging at these galaxies is not known, but it may be invisible matter clumped on much larger scales than can be readily explained by any current theory." Each new discovery, made possible by another theory and another method of observation and measurement, opens us to yet another unknown. We give names to our discoveries, and in the naming make things real. But beyond conditioned thought, we realize that all is story. The poet Muriel Rukeyser observed, "The universe is made of stories, not atoms." Or to say it another way, atoms are stories of our human comprehension of the universe. Even the universe, the idea of the universe, is a story we humans tell.

---

Renewal may come. But the overall sense of life at the age of sixty-one is one of loss. When an observer noted the personal pain in my presentation of a week or so ago, I replied that it is the pain of being alive. In our aging, we carry with us the accumulation of the losses over the years. Easy now to despair as we grow into death.

Yesterday's newspaper carried the obituary of May Sarton. Poet, novelist, my inspiration for years, she died last Sunday of breast cancer at the age of eighty-three. In a series of journals, all published as books, May Sarton documented her last years of living in a house near the ocean in Maine. I might not be keeping my own daily accounts if I had not read *Journal of Solitude*, *Recovering*, *At Seventy*, *After the Stroke*, *Endgame*, and *Encore*. She wrote of the struggle to create a life, to be alive, and of the rewards of a solitary life. She wrote, "Loneliness is most acutely felt with other people, for with others, even with a lover sometimes, we suffer from our differences—differences of taste, temperament, mood."

Quietly, with patience, tending her garden as long as her failing health permitted, May Sarton waited for the moment to come "when the world falls away." In an interview, speaking about her "self-imposed loneliness," she said, "Music itself can only be heard alone. Solitude is the salt of personhood. It brings out the authentic flavor of every experience." She added, "Alone we can afford to be wholly whatever we are, and to feel whatever we feel absolutely."

And yet, and always the yet, May Sarton wrote two years later in her "Winter Thoughts": "We have got to warm ourselves back to the certainty that it is only when we lose the connection between ourselves and other people that we begin to freeze up into despair. That connection has to be kept open whatever happens. It is kept open by letters, by unexpected encounters, or by simply contemplating the points of light here or there."

———

Winter has come and snow is falling outside my window this January morning. It is time to end this little requiem. There are other things to do. A writing that is less personal seems to be in order, something that is not written in the first person.

Imagine the music that continues to play as a requiem for the living and the dead. All morning long the living room has been filled with music. Duke Ellington has played a memorial to his friend, composer and arranger Billy Strayhorn, in the album *And His Mother Called Him Bill.* I am haunted especially by Ellington's solo piano on "Lotus Blossom." I listen to Hank Jones's tribute to his brother in "Upon Reflection." Miles Davis plays "My Funny Valentine," thinking about the death of John Kennedy, in the live performance at Lincoln Center in 1964. Frank Sinatra sings sixteen songs of love and loss on the album *In the Wee Small Hours of the Morning.*

This afternoon, as the winter storm continues, I look forward to hearing Haydn's Symphony No. 98, composed in 1792, an elegiac response to the news of Mozart's death. I will end the afternoon with one of Beethoven's late string quartets, No. 15 in A minor. I will listen carefully to the third movement, marked *Molto adagio,* Beethoven's hymn of gratitude for recovery from a long illness. In the evening, I will study Gustav Mahler's Ninth Symphony. For what more could one wish? Grace is everywhere.

# *Acknowledgment*

Grateful acknowledgment is made to the following colleagues for their comments and encouragement: Arthur Bochner, Steve Delchamps, Norman Denzin, Carolyn Ellis, Ronald Farrell, John Galliher, Douglas Harper, Martha Huggins, Richard Jones, Dragan Milovanovic, Harold Pepinsky, and Allen Shelton. And for printing my photographs, my thanks to Paul Clark.

# *Bibliography*

Adams, Robert. *Beauty in Photography: Essays in Defense of Traditional Values*. New York: Aperature, 1981.

Agee, James, and Walker Evans. *Let Us Now Praise Famous Men*. Boston: Houghton Mifflin, 1988 [1939].

Ashbery, John. *Hotel Lautréamont*. New York: Alfred A. Knopf.

Auden, W. H. *Collected Poems*. Edited by Edward Mendelson. New York: Vintage Books, 1991.

Bailey, Martin, editor. *Van Gogh: Letters from Provence*. New York: Clarkson N. Potter, 1990.

Barthes, Roland. *Camera Lucida: Reflections on Photography*. Translated by Richard Howard. New York: Hill and Wang, 1981.

Bashō, Matsuo. *The Narrow Road to the Deep North and Other Travel Essays*. Translated by Nobuyuki Yuasa. New York: Penguin, 1966.

Beckett, Samuel. *Stories and Texts for Nothing*. Translated by Richard Seaver. New York: Grove Press, 1970.

Benjamin, Walter. "The Work of Art in the Age of Reproduction." In *Illuminations*. New York: Schocken, 1969 [1936].

Bergman, Ingmar. *Images: My Life in Film*. Translated by Marianne Ruuth. New York: Arcade, 1994.

Bernanos, Georges. *The Diary of a Country Priest*. Translated by Pamela Morris. New York: Carroll and Greb Publishers, 1983 [1937].

Berry, Wendell. *Harlan Hubbard: Life and Work*. New York: Parthenon, 1990.

*Bhagavad Gita, The*. Translated by Eknath Easwaran. Petaluma, Cal.: Nilgiri Press, 1985.

Bowles, Paul. *Days: Tangier Journal, 1987–1989*. New York: Ecco Press, 1991.

Burke, Edmund. *A Philosophical Enquiry into the Origin of Our Ideas of the Sublime and Beautiful*. Edited by J.T. Boulton. Reprint. London: Routledge and Kegan Paul, 1958 [1857].

Burton, Robert. *The Anatomy of Melancholy*. Eighth edition. Philadelphia: J.W. Moore, 1857.

Byron, Thomas. *The Heart of Awareness: A Translation of the Ashtavakra Gita*. Boston: Shambhala, 1990.

Camus, Albert. *American Journals*. Translated by Hugh Levick. New York: Paragon House, 1987.

———. *The Fall*. Translated by Justin O'Brien. New York: Vintage Books, 1956.

———. *The Myth of Sisyphus and Other Essays*. Translated by Justin O'Brien. New York: Alfred A. Knopf, 1955.

———. *The Stranger*. Translated by Matthew Ward. New York: Alfred A. Knopf, 1993 [1946].

Cardenal, Ernesto. "Death of Thomas Merton." In *A Merton Celebration*. Edited by Deba Patnaik. Notre Dame: Ave Marie Press, 1981.

Cavell, Stanley. "Introduction" to "Exile, Alienation, and Estrangement," *Social Research* 58 (Spring 1991): 9–10.

Cioran, E. M. *The Temptation to Exist*. Translated by Richard Howard. Chicago: Quadrangle Books, 1968.

———. *The Trouble with Being Born*. Translated by Richard Howard. Viking Press, 1976.

Cleary, Thomas, editor and translator. *Rational Zen: The Mind of Dōgen Zenji*. Boston: Shambhala, 1992.

———, editor and translator. *Zen Essences: The Science of Freedom*. Boston: Shambhala, 1989.

Cohen-Solal, Annie. *Sartre: A Life*. Translated by Anne Cancogni. New York: Pantheon Books, 1987.

Coleman, Francis X. J. *Neither Angel nor Beast: the Life and Work of Blaise Pascal*. New York: Routledge and Kegan Paul, 1986.

Cook, Francis H. *Sounds of Valley Streams: Enlightenment in Dōgen's Zen*. Albany: State University of New York Press, 1989.

Daniélou, Alain. *The Way of the Labyrinth*. Translated by Marie-Claire Cournand. New York: New Directions, 1987.

*Dhammapada, The*. Translated by Eknath Easwaran. Petaluma, Cal.: Nilgiri Press, 1985.

Dunaway, David King. *Huxley in Hollywood*. New York: Harper & Row, 1989.

Durcan, Paul. *Crazy About Women*. Dublin: The National Gallery of Ireland, 1991.

Dürckheim, Karlfried Graf. "The Voice of the Master," *Parabola* 15 (August 1990):4–12.

Eckhart, Meister. *Meister Eckhart: A Modern Translation*. Translated by Raymond Bernard Blakney. New York: Harper, 1957.

Eliot, T. S. *Four Quartets*. New York: Harcourt Brace Jovanovich, 1971.

Emerson, Ralph Waldo. "Nature." In *Selected Writings of Ralph Waldo Emerson*. Edited by William H. Gilman. New York: New American Library, 1965.

Fromm, Erich. *The Art of Loving*. New York: Harper & Row, 1989 [1956].

———. *To Have or To Be?* New York: Harper & Row, 1976.

Goethe, Johann Wolfgang von. *Italian Journey, 1786–1788*. Translated by W.H. Auden and Elizabeth Mayer. San Francisco: North Point Press, 1982.

Goldstein, Joseph, and Jack Kornfield. *Seeking the Heart of Wisdom*. Boston: Shambhala, 1987.

Goodrich, Lloyd. *Edward Hopper*. New York: Harry N. Abrams, 1983.

Griffin, John Howard. *The Hermitage Journals*. Edited by Conger Beasley. Kansas City: Andrews and McMeel, 1981.

Griffiths, Bede. *The Cosmic Revelation: the Hindu Way to God*. Springfield, Ill.: Templegate Publishers, 1983.

———. *The Golden String.* Springfield, Ill.: Templegate Publishers, 1980.

Hammarskjöld, Dag. *Markings.* Translated by Leif Sjöberg and W. H. Auden. New York: Alfred A. Knopf, 1964.

Hanh, Thich Nhat. *Being Peace.* Berkeley: Parallax Press, 1987.

———. *The Heart of Understanding: Commentaries on the Prayñaparamita Heart Sutra.* Berkeley: Parallax Press, 1988.

———. *Peace is Every Step.* New York: Bantam Books, 1991.

———. "Birth, Death and Interbeing," *Karuna* 8 (Spring 1991): 3–6.

Harper, Ralph. *On Presence: Variations and Reflections.* Philadelphia: Trinity Press International, 1991.

Herbert, Zbigniew. *Still Life With Bridle.* Translated by John and Bogdana Carpenter. Hopewell, N.J.: Ecco Press, 1991.

Hokanson, Drake. *The Lincoln Highway: Mainstreet Across America.* Iowa City: University of Iowa Press, 1988.

Huxley, Aldous. *Island.* New York: Harper & Brothers, 1962.

Jackson, Michael. *At Home in the World.* Durham: Duke University Press, 1995.

Johnston, William. *The Inner Eye of Love: Mysticism and Religion.* San Francisco: Harper & Row, 1978.

Joyce, James. "The Dead." In *Dubliners.* New York: Viking Penguin, 1976 [1916].

Kafka, Franz. *The Castle.* Translated by Willa Muir and Edwin Muir. New York: Alfred A. Knopf, 1992 [1926].

———. *Selected Short Stories of Franz Kafka.* Translated by Willa Muir and Edwin Muir. New York: Random House, 1980.

Kant, Immanuel. *Critique of Judgement.* New York: Hafner Press, 1951 [1790].

Kapleau, Philip. *The Wheel of Life and Death.* New York: Doubleday, 1989.

Kierkegaard, Søren. *The Diary of Søren Kierkegaard.* Edited by Peter P. Rohde, New York: Philosophical Library, 1960.

Kinser, Samuel. "Research, Teaching, Citizenship," *Faculty Bulletin* (Northern Illinois University) 58 (September 1994): 23–26.

Koerner, Joseph Leo. *Caspar David Friedrich and the Subject of Landscape.* New Haven: Yale University Press, 1990.

Kundera, Milan. *The Art of the Novel.* London: Faber and Faber, 1988.

Lagerkvist, Pär. *Evening Land.* Translated by W.H. Auden and Leif Sjoberg. Detroit: Wayne State University Press, 1975.

Lahr, John. "Brian Friel's Blind Faith," *The New Yorker*, October 17, 1994, pp. 107–10.

Lao-Tzu. *Tao Te Ching.* Translated by Stephen Mitchell. New York: Harper & Row, 1988.

Lawrence, D. H. *Mornings in Mexico.* Salt Lake City: Gibbs M. Smith, 1982 [1927].

Lefebvre, Henri. "The Everyday and Everydayness." Translated by Christine Levich. In *Yale French Studies*, number 73 (1987): 7–11.

Lehrman, Fredric. *The Sacred Landscape.* Berkeley: Celestial Arts, 1988.

Maezremi, Hakruyu Taizan. *The Way of Everyday Life.* Los Angeles: Zen Center, 1978.

Matthiessen, Peter. *The Snow Leopard.* New York: Viking, 1978.

McLuhan, T. D. *Touch the Earth: A Self-Portrait of Indian Experience.* New York: Simon and Schuster, 1971.

Merton, Thomas. *The Asian Journal of Thomas Merton.* New York: New Directions, 1973.

———. *The Silent Life.* New York: Farrar, Straus and Giroux.

———. *Thoughts on Solitude.* New York: Farrar, Straus and Giroux, 1958.

———. *The Waters of Siloe.* New York: Harcourt Brace Jovanovich, 1949.

———. *The Way of Chuang Tzu.* New York: New Directions, 1965.

———. *The Wisdom of the Desert.* New York: New Directions, 1960.

Mikolaycak, Charles. *Orpheus.* New York: Harcourt Brace Jovanovich, 1992.

Mitchell, Stephen. *The Gospel According to Jesus*. New York: HarperCollins, 1991.

Montaigne, Michel De. *The Complete Essays of Montaigne*. Translated by Donald M. Frame. Palo Alto: Stanford University Press, 1958.

Morris, Wright. *Photographs and Words*. Edited by James Alinder. New York: Friends of Photography, 1982.

Mott, Thomas. *The Seven Mountains of Thomas Merton*. Boston: Houghton Mifflin, 1984.

Nietzsche, Friedrich. *The Gay Science*. Translated by Walter Kaufmann. New York: Vintage Books, 1974.

———. *Thus Spoke Zarathustra*. Translated by Walter Kaufmann. New York: Viking. 1978 [1892].

O'Connell, Michael. *Robert Burton*. Boston: Twayne, 1986.

*Primer on Monastic Spirituality*. Dubuque: New Melleray Abbey, nd.

Quinney, Laura. *Literary Power and the Criteria of Truth*. Gainesville: University Press of Florida, 1995.

Quinney, Richard. *Journey to a Far Place*. Philadelphia: Temple University Press, 1991.

Reps, Paul, compiled. *Zen Flesh, Zen Bones*. New York: Viking Penguin, 1971.

Rewald, Sabine, editor. *The Romantic Version of Caspar David Friedrich*. New York: The Metropolitan Museum of Art, 1990.

Richardson, Robert D., Jr. *Henry Thoreau: A Life of the Mind*. Berkeley: University of California Press, 1986.

Rilke, Rainer Maria. *Letters to a Young Poet*. Translated by Stephen Mitchell. New York: Random House, 1984.

———. *The Selected Poetry of Rainer Maria Rilke*. Edited and translated by Stephen Mitchell. New York: Random House, 1982.

Roberts, Elizabeth, and Elias Amidon, editors. *Earth Prayers: From Around the World, 365 Prayers, Psalms, and Invocations for Honoring the Earth*. New York: Harper Collins, 1991.

Ryōkan. *One Robe, One Bowl: The Zen Poetry of Ryōkan*. Translated by John Stevens. New York: Weatherhill, 1977.

Sarton, May. *Endgame: A Journal of the Seventy-Ninth Year*. New York: W. W. Norton, 1992.

Sartre, Jean-Paul. *Nausea*. Translated by Lloyd Alexander. New York: New Directions, 1964.

Seung, Sahn. *Only Don't Know*. San Francisco: Four Seasons Foundation, 1982.

Shelley, Percy Bysshe. "Mont Blanc." In *Selected Poetry and Prose*. New York: Routledge, 1991.

Stafford, William. *Stories That Could Be True: New and Collected Poems*. New York: Harper & Row, 1977.

———. *Writing the Australian Crawl*. Ann Arbor: University of Michigan Press, 1978.

Steiner, George. *Real Presences*. Chicago: University of Chicago Press, 1989.

Sudek, Josef. *Josef Sudek, Poet of Prague: A Photographer's Life*. Biographical Profile by Anna Farova. New York: Aperture, 1990.

Szarkowski, John. *Looking at Photographs*. New York: The Museum of Modern Art, 1973.

Thiele, Leslie Paul. "Twilight of Modernity: Nietzsche, Heidegger, and Politics," *Political Theory* 22 (August 1994): 468–90.

Thoreau, Henry D. *Walden*. Edited by J. Lyndon Shanley. Princeton: Princeton University Press, 1973.

Twitchell, James B. *Romantic Horizons: Aspects of the Sublime in English Poetry and Painting, 1770–1850*. Columbia: University of Missouri Press, 1983.

*Upanishads, The*. Translated by Eknath Easwaran. Petaluma, Cal.: Nilgiri Press, 1987.

Vicari, E. Patricia. *The View From Minerva's Tower: Learning and Imagination in The Anatomy of Melancholy*. Toronto: University of Toronto Press, 1989.

Wang, Wei. *Laughing Lost in the Mountains: Poems of Wang Wei*. Translated by Tony Barnstone, Willis Barnstone, and Xu Haixin. Hanover: University Press of New England, 1991.

Watts, Alan. *The Way of Liberation: Essays and Lectures on the Transformation of Self.* Edited by Mark Watts and Rebecca Shropshire. New York: Weatherhill, 1983.

White, E.B. *One Man's Meat.* New York: Harper & Row, 1982.

White, Minor. *Minor White: Rites & Passages.* Biographical Essay by James Becker Hall. New York: Aperture, 1978.

Wilton, Andrew. *Turner and the Sublime.* London: British Museum Publications, 1980.

Wittgenstein, Ludwig. *Tractatus Logico-Philosophicus.* Translated by C.K. Ogden. London: Routledge and Kegan Paul, 1981.

Young, Edward. *Night Thoughts.* Edinburgh: James Nichol, 1853.